This book was made possible through
the generous assistance of:

 Eastman Kodak Co.

Nikon

NORTHWEST AIRLINES

Bank America Corporation
WorldMoney Travelers Cheques

Holiday Inn
Lido Beijing
北京丽都假日饭店

First published 1989 by Collins Publishers, Inc.,
San Francisco

Copyright © 1989 by Collins Publishers, Inc.

Library of Congress Cataloging-in-Publication Data
Main entry under title: A Day in the Life of China.

ISBN 0-00-215321-1
1. China–Description and Travel–1976–Views.
2. China–Social life and customs–1976–Pictorial Works.
I. Cohen, David, 1955–

DS712.D39 1989
951.05'8'0222   89–10034

Project Director: David Cohen
Art Director: Jennifer Barry

Printed in Japan   First printing July 1989
10 9 8 7 6 5 4 3 2 1

A Day in the Life of China

**Photographed by 90 of the
world's leading photojournalists
on one day, April 15, 1989**

Collins Publishers

This book was published by Collins Publishers in association with
Weldon Owen Publishing, the China National Publishing Industry Trading Corporation and
the Great Wall Publishing House. Due to a difference of opinion about the inclusion
of certain photographs and text, our Chinese partners have made a formal request to withdraw from this
cooperative effort. We gratefully acknowledge their invaluable contribution to this book and
look forward to the time when our association can be renewed.

Leshan, 6:30 AM: Loaded down with sugar cane,
a Sichuan farmer walks slowly through the morning fog.
Photographer: **Neal Ulevich, USA**

Kunming, 7:00 AM: Early morning at the Number Three Kindergarten.
Photographer: **Sarah Leen, USA**

Xiahe, 7:15 AM: At the Labrang Monastery in southern
Gansu, Tibetan monks rehearse a centuries-old mask dance.
Photographer: **Dilip Mehta, Canada**

Beijing, 7:30 AM: On the morning of April 15, thousands of
Flying Pigeon bicycles passed before Mao and the Forbidden City.
Photographer: **David Hume Kennerly, USA**

China has fascinated the Western world since the early days of the Han dynasty, when Roman traders first ventured forth on the Silk Road across the High Pamirs. *China*. The name itself evokes images of bat-winged fishing junks, temples thick with incense, Mongolian ponies flying across the steppe and broad avenues packed with bicycles.

Inspired by these and other romantic visions of exotic Cathay, 90 of the world's leading photojournalists fanned out across China on April 15, 1989. Their assignment: capture the life of the country on film in a single 24-hour period; make extraordinary pictures of ordinary events.

In fact, April 15 turned out to be far from ordinary. The photographers found a country caught up in a whirlwind of economic, social and political change. Bucolic temples now sat in Special Economic Zones bustling with commercial activity. Stonewashed Levi's and designer fashions had replaced the once ubiquitous Mao suit. Students, exposed to outside ideas and influences, were openly questioning the government.

By the end of *A Day in the Life of China*, it seemed that the very foundations of Chinese society were shifting. As the photographers were winding up their last assignments, volatile political forces were building rapidly. By the following afternoon, *Day in the Life* photographers returning to Beijing found the first of one million students and workers assembling in Tiananmen Square demanding democracy and an end to corruption. Their seven-week occupation of China's symbolic heart would capture the whole world's attention. The sudden and tragic conflict that followed would shock people everywhere.

On October 1, 1989, the People's Republic of China celebrated its 40th anniversary. In those four decades it has experienced tumultuous change on a regular basis–the Hundred Flowers Campaign, the Great Leap Forward, the Cultural Revolution, the fall of the Gang of Four. By all indications, the next 40 years will be equally momentous. This book makes no attempt at prophesy. It is merely a portrait of a single day–a day packed with the anomalies and commotion that are part and parcel of modern China. But if it is possible to divine the future by observing the present, then the photographic odyssey contained herein is worthy of study. There *are* instants in time when it is possible to see history being made. April 15, 1989 seemed to be such a day.

— David DeVoss

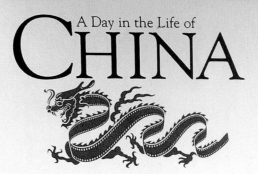

A Day in the Life of

CHINA

February 1, 1989

Mr. Douglas Menuez
85 Liberty Ship Way
Sausalito, California 94965

Dear Doug,

It gives us great pleasure to invite you to participate in *A Day in the Life of China*. Like previous *Day in the Life* projects, this will be a challenging and wonderfully memorable experience. Unlike previous projects, this is China.

Since the dawn of history, China has been a world apart—a gargantuan social and cultural entity that has purposefully kept to itself. For the past 15 years, however, the doors have been opening slowly. China and the rest of the world are becoming acquainted. No one can predict what effect this cultural and economic bartering will have. We do know, however, that we are presented with a rare opportunity to document a vast and ancient civilization in the midst of profound change.

To mark the 40th anniversary of the founding of the People's Republic, the government has agreed to cooperate in the publication of *A Day in the Life of China*. This means that after months of negotiation, we have been granted unprecedented access to all Chinese provinces and Autonomous Regions. To accomplish this required the support of many talented and dedicated people at Weldon Owen Publishing in Hong Kong, and at the Great Wall Publishing House, the People's Liberation Army and the Chinese National Publishing Industry Trading Corporation in Beijing. The project has also benefitted tremendously from the support of several corporate sponsors and the guidance of a distinguished group of picture editors, including:

Sandra Eisert, *The San Jose Mercury News*   Michael Rand, *The London Sunday Times*
Alfonso Gutiérrez Escera, *A.G.E. Fotostock*   Dieter Steiner, *Stern Magazine (Germany)*
Peter Howe, *Life Magazine*   Susan Vermazen, *New York Magazine*
Eliane Laffont, Sygma   Michele Stephenson, *Time Magazine*
Michele McNally, *Fortune Magazine*   George Wedding, *The Sacramento Bee*
Robert Pledge, Contact Press Images

Collins Publishers   50 Osgood Place   San Francisco, CA 94133   (415) 788-4111   Fax: (415) 788-3651   Telex: 6501343670 MCI

Perhaps more than ever before, hundreds of people are doing everything in their power to provide the access and assistance you will need to create important pictures and an important book. Still, it all comes down to the photographs you take: Your hard work, your skill and your vision on a single day—Saturday, April 15, 1989.

The schedule: On Sunday, April 9, you and 60 photojournalists from 15 countries will arrive in Hong Kong. On Monday, April 10, you will fly to Beijing, joining a team of 29 top photographers from the PRC. That evening, all photographers will gather for an initial briefing, followed by a welcoming banquet hosted by Nikon. The next day, you will assemble for a group portrait in Tiananmen Square and take part in Kodak's photography workshop for Chinese schoolchildren. Finally, you will be wined and dined at a banquet hosted by Kodak and our Chinese partners before setting out for your assignment. On April 16 and 17 you will return to Beijing, drop off your film, attend a farewell gathering, overnight and then fly to Hong Kong for your connecting flights home.

The sponsors of *A Day in the Life of China*—Eastman Kodak, Nikon, Northwest Airlines, BankAmerica Corp.\WorldMoney Travelers Cheques, Holiday Inn Lido and Federal Express—understand that the participants in this project are journalists, and they have agreed, without exception, not to exert influence over the editorial process. As with our previous projects, we have no intention of producing a travelogue or a collection of postcards. Our goal is to create a visual time capsule, and you can rest assured that every aspect of picture selection, text, design, production and publicity will be carried out in a spirit of professionalism and creativity.

If you decide to accept our invitation, we ask that you first read the enclosed forms and contract carefully. These materials must be returned to us no later than February 10, 1989. We enclose a Federal Express envelope for your convenience. If for any reason you are unable to join us, please call Jennifer Erwitt as soon as possible.

Documenting the world's most-populous nation in a single day is obviously a colossal task—especially in a place where transportation, lodging and communications can be entirely unpredictable. We can't guarantee that your assignment will be smooth or luxurious—in fact, we predict that a few photographers will never make it to their assigned areas. We do promise, however, that *A Day in the Life of China* will be a great adventure. I hope to see you in Hong Kong on April 9.

Best regards,

David Cohen
Project Director

● *Left*

On the morning of April 15, 1989, the population of the People's Republic of China officially reached 1.1 billion.
Photographer:
David Hume Kennerly, USA

● *Above*

Early morning *tai ji quan* gives way to the tango at Ritan Park in Beijing.
Photographer:
Paul Chesley, USA

● *Following page*

Bicycle commuters make their way across the Haizhu Bridge on a rainy Saturday morning in Guangzhou. Known as Canton in the West, the city's streets are among the most crowded in China–largely due to an influx of rural job seekers. Lured by South China's booming economy and Guangzhou's proximity to Hong Kong, more than a million people poured into the area during one three-week period in February 1989.
Photographer:
Gerd Ludwig, W. Germany

● *Left*

Rice planting in Pingwu: China produces 7,000 varieties of rice. All require back-breaking labor. Initially, seed is scattered and allowed to grow for approximately one month in specially prepared beds. Then the seedlings are uprooted and transplanted in small clusters to larger paddy fields. Although the work is grueling, peasants are well compensated. They can easily earn triple the salary of many factory workers, and five times the amount paid to a university professor.

Photographer:

Michael Bryant, USA

● *Above*

Every spring, Qiang peasants in northern Sichuan face the arduous task of fertilizing their hillside terraces. Entire villages are mobilized to haul 100-pound tubs of manure up from the valley floor. The peasants pictured here are just beginning their six-mile trek–all uphill.

Photographer:

Yuan Xuejun, China

Since Mao Zedong died at the age of 82 in 1976, more than 52 million Chinese have filed through his mausoleum at the south end of Tiananmen Square. The former Communist Party chairman's remains lie in a crystal sarcophagus behind a lobby dominated by his seated statue. In early 1989, observers reported that his remains (known to the irreverent as "peasant under glass") seem to be shrinking. But Mao's personal physician, Dr. Xu Jing, who monitors the Great Helmsman in death as in life, says his patient is well preserved.
Photographer:
David Hume Kennerly, USA

These fishermen in Guangxi must stand on two-foot stilts to avoid the sharp rocks and shells on the ocean floor.
Photographer:
Claus C. Meyer, W. Germany

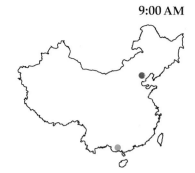

● *Left*

At a rural elementary school in the northern town of Yulin, first graders are introduced to some of the 140,000 characters that make up the Chinese lexicon. Before the 1949 revolution, schooling often consisted of rote memorization of Confucian classics. The People's Republic broadened educational opportunities, but the quality of instruction remains low. Illiteracy by some measures runs to 20 percent in the cities and is much higher in the countryside.
Photographer:
Stephanie Maze, USA

● *Above*

Honor students Dong Yintao and Li Xiaohao log on at the Number Three Grammar School in Wuhan. Since there is only one computer for every 15,000 people in China, their opportunity is a rare one.
Photographer:
Randy Olson, USA

● *Right*

Chen Meifang is one of seven students attending the one-room village school in Gang-chong, Qinghai. The eighth child in the village can't go to school because his parents are unable to afford the yearly five-yuan ($1.35) fee for books.
Photographer:
Li Qianguang, China

● *Left*

First-graders at a Dachang primary school sing "Unity is good; collectivism is good" before taking their morning nap.
Photographer:
Rick Rickman, USA

● *Above*

Potty training: Despite the hovering presence of her teacher (and a *Day in the Life* photographer), this young girl in a Ehotan day-care center will not be rushed.
Photographer:
Jim Richardson, USA

● *Following page*

Two thousand technicians work at a television assembly facility in Wuxi. They make 30 different kinds of black-and-white and color televisions under the brand name Hongmei. The factory's motto: "Customer supreme, reputation first."
Photographer:
Volker Hinz, W. Germany

● *Left*

Prior to his death in 1976, Mao Zedong's image was ubiquitous. Today, one of the few public places his portrait still appears is on the Gate of Heavenly Peace in Tiananmen Square—the spot where he proclaimed the birth of the People's Republic on October 1, 1949. Some years ago, it was proposed that the famous visage be taken down, but that now seems unlikely. The formidable painting is still a popular attraction for Chinese and foreign visitors alike.
Photographer:
David Hume Kennerly, USA

● *Above*

With a population of 13 million, Shanghai is among China's most crowded cities. Despite the efforts of a corps of masked street sweepers, it is also among the dirtiest. Due to the extensive use of coal and diesel fuel, every square mile of the city is blanketed by more than 70 tons of soot every month.
Photographer:
Doug Menuez, USA

● *Left*

At the Khotan Silk Factory in
Xinjiang, nimble-fingered
Uighur women loosen silk
strands from cocoons and feed
them onto spinning reels. The
finest silk comes from captive
worms fed a continuous diet
of chopped mulberry leaves.
About one thousand of their
cocoons are needed to make
a typical woman's blouse.
Photographer:
Jim Richardson, USA

● *Above*

Merchants, scholars and even government fish buyers, like this man in the port of Shen-jiamen, have relied on the abacus since the 15th century. On an abacus, basic math is a breeze; even square roots are no sweat. In competition against an electronic calculator the abacus usually loses, but not by much.

Photographer:

Chen Changfen, China

● *Right*

Chinese fashions used to come in two colors: dark blue and dark green. Now bright pastels, colorful prints and synthetic knits can be found in free-enterprise markets throughout the country.

Photographer:

Diego Goldberg, Argentina

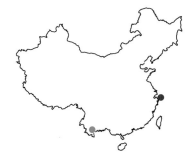

The state-run shoe store in Wenzhou may not offer the latest styles, but the average price is only $8 a pair. Shoes purchased from private hawkers can cost 50 percent more, but tend to be more fashionable.
Photographer:
Sam Garcia, USA

During the Han dynasty, emperors discovered that oysters brought north from the tropical Beibu Gulf often contained large pearls with a lustrous, pink luminescence. Thirteen centuries later, the Ming emperor Hongwu sent a palace eunuch along with 3,000 conscripts to begin producing cultured pearls. The process begins with the "seeding" of selected oysters. Then the oysters are placed into net pouches and suspended from wooden scaffolds so that tides rich in nutrients may continually wash over them. Because the water temperature is warmer, pearls cultured here are generally larger than those from Japan.
Photographer:
Claus C. Meyer, W. Germany

● *Above*

Protected from the semitropical sun, Beibu Gulf oyster farmers inspect the crop. It is not un-common for a single oyster to contain several pearls.
Photographer:
Claus C. Meyer, W. Germany

● *Above*

Here on Fujian's Dazuo Peninsula, hauling 200-pound blocks of granite is traditionally women's work. The people who run the quarries once considered buying modern hauling equipment. The women objected. Even work this arduous was better than possible unemployment.
Photographer:
Guy Le Querrec, France

Since rice is more water-tolerant than weeds, the Chinese flood their paddies instead of using herbicides. Improved methods of cultivation and the use of hybrid grains have kept food production ahead of population growth. But with only 11 percent of the total land arable–compared to almost 25 percent in the United States–there is constant pressure to increase yields.
Photographer:
Don Cochran, USA

South of Shanghai, in the city of Shaoxing, deliverymen avoid highway gridlock in black *wupeng* boats. The manpowered *wupeng* cruise thousands of tributaries that feed into the Grand Canal, an engineering wonder equal in scale to the Great Wall itself.
Photographer:
Chen Changfen, China

The sparkling Daning River runs from the mountains of Sichuan down to the mighty Yangtse. Here, it meanders around the town of Wuxi. Like most Chinese river towns, Wuxi is laid out in accordance with the ancient principles of *fengshui:* back to the mountain, face to the water.
Photographer:
Rick Rickman, USA

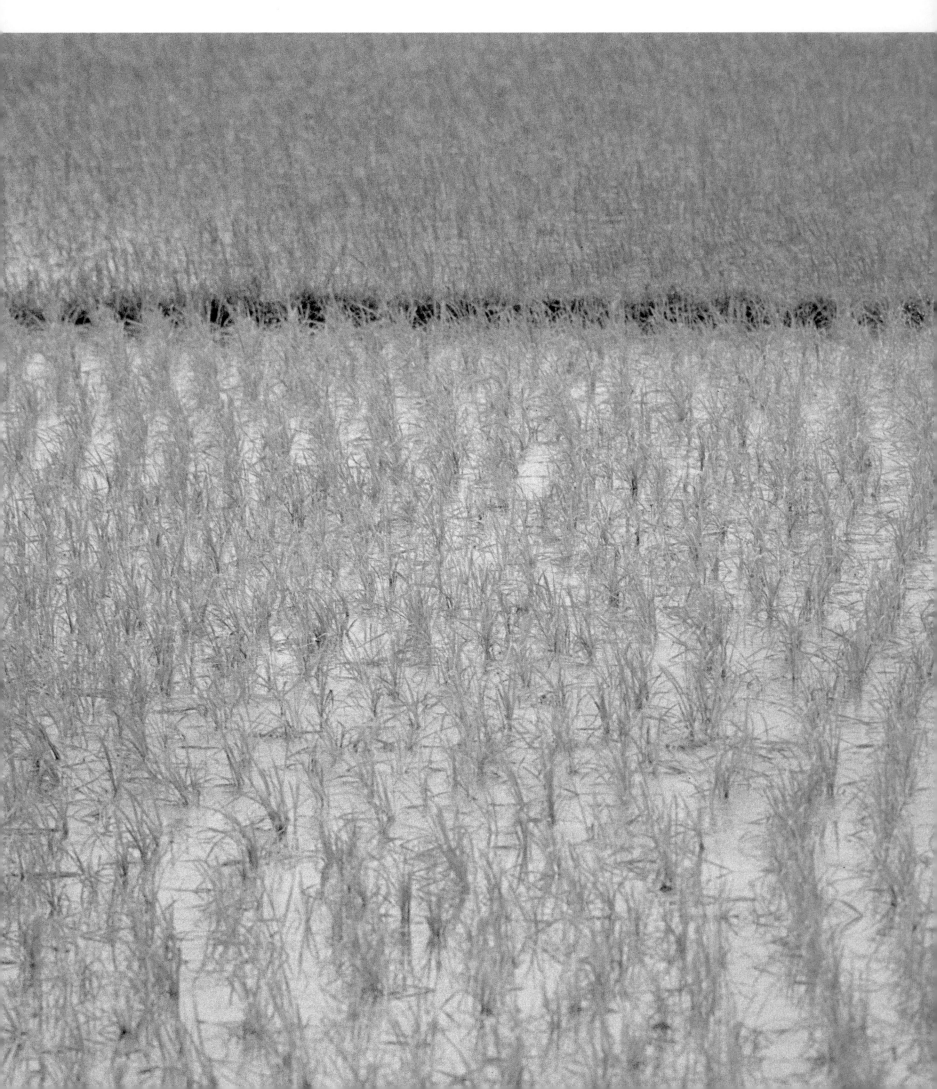

● *Above*

The Longsheng area of Guangxi
is famed for its dramatic dragon-
backed rice terraces. Rising 3,000
feet from the valley floor, the
paddy fields are the result of 18
generations of toil by the
Zhuang minority people. An
intricate irrigation system of
bamboo pipes keeps the terraces
well watered. Productivity remains low, however, since most
of the narrow terraces must be
cultivated without oxen.
Photographer:
Joe Rossi, USA

● *Above*

Air force pilots stationed near Xi'an practice maneuvers on an aerial map of the region. The pilot in the foreground is crouching at the convergence of the Yellow River and its principal tributary, the Wei. Later in the day, the map doubles as a basketball court.
Photographer:
Wu Zhiyi, China

● *Left*

Excedrin headache number 304: Assisted by a willing drill instructor, marine recruits in Zhanjiang practice *ying qigong*, a breathing and mind control exercise that makes them impervious to injury and pain.
Photographer:
Long Yunhe, China

● *Above*

At the Kaifeng Police Academy, cadets endure a sequence of gut-rending calisthenics. To help the Chinese police better their law enforcement skills, China's Public Security Ministry hired a former police chief from Milpitas, California, as an adviser. During his first police science class, he showed the movie *Dirty Harry*.
Photographer:
Li Binbin, China

● *Above*

This 18-month-old Chengdu youngster is riding a character known in China as Tang Lao Ya or "Old Duck Tang." Tang and his friend "Old Mouse Mi" can be seen all over China.
Photographer:
George Steinmetz, USA

● *Above*

Originally built for postal carriers by the Ministry of Posts and Telecommunications, Jialing motorcycles from Chongqing are popular with everyone because of their payload capacity.
Photographer:
Neal Ulevich, USA

● *Left*

Rice is as central to China's culture as it is to its cuisine. The very word for rice, *fan*, is synonomous with food itself. Instead of saying hello, the Chinese will often greet each other with the words, *Chi fan le mei you*, which means, "Have you eaten rice yet?" When the government of Deng Xiaoping did away with guaranteed lifetime employment it was known as "breaking the iron rice bowl."
Photographer:
Raphaël Gaillarde, France

● *Below*

Warm weather affords this
family in Fujian an opportunity
to enjoy their lunch *al fresco*.
Photographer:
David Alan Harvey, USA

● *Above*

Even Chinese children have difficulty learning to eat with chopsticks. The frustration is compounded when you can't swallow what you finally pick up. Protected from Beijing's dusty air by gauze bags, these two toddlers want the lesson to end and lunch to begin.
Photographer:
Paul Chesley, USA

● *Right*

A Beijing bicycle commuter uses a net scarf to protect herself from dust blowing off the Gobi Desert 150 miles away.
Photographer:
Paul Chesley, USA

● *Left*

All steamed up: Getting a "perm" in Luoyang can be a real ordeal. Once the curlers are in place, beauticians at this unisex hair salon set the style with steaming hot towels.
Photographer:
Robin Moyer, USA

● *Above*

A performer in a traveling opera troupe prepares for an evening performance in Jiangxi. Roles in Chinese opera are highly codified. The clothes and makeup of this actress denote that she will be playing a refined young woman.
Photographer:
Jean-Pierre Laffont, France

● *Following page*

Exchanging secrets: In the remote Moslem city of Kashgar, many Uighur women wear veils whenever they go outside.
Photographer:
Bruno Barbey, France

Ge Pengren's penchant for
nude portraiture has made him
one of Beijing's more contro-
versial artists. He is, however,
only the most recent painter to
test the limits of artistic license.
In the Ming period (1368-1644),
painters were prohibited from
rendering nudes, and made
sexual innuendos by discreetly
adding copulating insects in
the background foliage. Risqué
Qing dynasty (1644-1911)
scroll painters relied on double
entendre. For example, the
term for embroider (*xiu*) is pro-
nounced the same way as an
obscure term for sexual intercourse. Hence, maidens
occupied with needlework
became a popular theme.
Photographer:
John Giannini, USA

Portraits of Tibet by **Steve McCurry, USA**

Three centuries ago, during the reign of the Qing emperor Kangxi, southwestern Fujian was plagued by gangs of roving bandits. To protect themselves, the Hakka people built dwellings large enough to shelter an entire clan. This four-story roundhouse outside Hukeng is more than 40 feet high and 725 feet around.

About 120 members of the Li clan still live in their ancestral fortress. They use the first floor for cooking and dining. Food and grain are stored on the second, while the third and fourth floors are divided into living rooms and bedrooms.
Photographer:
David Alan Harvey, USA

● *Right*

Most of the men awaiting trial
at the Jinhua municipal jail
stand accused of theft. In all
likelihood they will languish
for months because of a lawyer
shortage. The government
estimates that 500,000 lawyers
are needed to insure an ef-
ficient legal system. At present
China has only 33,000.
Photographer:
He Yanguang, China

● *Above and right*

April 15, 1989 was judgment day for Feng Jinjiang. As midday light poured into the Intermediate People's Court in Qingdao, the 19-year-old Shandong drifter was placed in the dock and accused of murdering a friend for $4.

Capital punishment is common in the People's Republic, though murderers are no longer beheaded on the spot as in pre-revolutionary days. *Photographer:* **Jim Mendenhall, USA**

審判长

審判

1:30 PM

Prisoners reconsider their crimes during a rehabilitation seminar inside the Luoyang municipal prison. When not atoning, these prisoners produce ersatz Tang-dynasty artifacts to be sold to tourists in Friendship Stores throughout the province.

Warden Wang Xuegong admits his is a no-frills prison, but with a recidivism rate below four percent and only one attempted escape in the past three years, he believes his methods are working.
Photographer:
Robin Moyer, USA

● *Left and above*

Monks at the Shaolin Temple in Henan demonstate the ancient art of *wushu*. Mistakenly called *kungfu* in the West, Chinese *wushu* dates from the sixth century B.C. According to temple historians, the discipline originated as an exercise for sedentary monks who spent most of their lives meditating. Patterned after the postures and actions of wild animals, *wushu* gained credibility in the seventh century when 13 fighting Shaolin monks saved a Tang emperor from attack. More recently, the People's Liberation Army has recruited Shaolin monks to train soldiers in hand-to-hand combat.
Photographer:
Bradley Clift, USA

● *Below*

A Saturday morning music class in Baotou, Inner Mongolia.
Photographer:
Nick Kelsh, USA

● *Following page*

While walking through an elementary school in Chang-chun, photographer Jerry Valente heard music coming from a classroom. "Thirty children were playing violins, but I was drawn to a very determined girl with glasses and a sweet face. I asked her to sit for a portrait, and she was very obliging, not at all shy or afraid. The light coming in through a back window was very soft. Her music teacher went to the art department for a piece of white cardboard that we used to bounce extra light. I loved her quiet expression and shot several rolls of film of her."
Photographer:
Jerry Valente, USA

● *Following page 97*

Child prodigies like Gao Hui, 13, often end up at the Shanghai Conservatory of Music. Central Asian musicians brought instruments much like her *pipa* to China in the second century B.C.
Photographer:
Doug Menuez, USA

● *Left*

In Wuqiao County, dining
room acrobatics like this have
always been considered per-
fectly normal. After all, Wuqiao
is to Chinese acrobatics what
Indiana is to basketball. Even
the peasants here pass the time
spinning plates, walking tight-
ropes and balancing pitchforks
on their foreheads. Acrobats
like Yu Yinghua and Yu
Shuangyan provide the region
with a major source of pride
as well as revenue.
Photographer:
Andy Levin, USA

● *Above*

Instead of a jump rope, many Chinese kids use a large, elastic loop six to twelve feet in diameter. Three players stretch the loop into a triangle while others jump through the center without touching the elastic. The loop is slowly raised until the last agile jumper is declared the winner.
Photographer:
Patrick Tehan, USA

● *Right*

The curio shop behind Mao's mausoleum does not sell replicas of the Great Helmsman. However, they do a brisk business in these toy cameras, each of which contains a half dozen scenic views of Beijing.
Photographer:
David Hume Kennerly, USA

Pics are for kids. On Saturday, April 15th, Kodak outfitted 200 schoolchildren with S.300 35mm cameras. In exchange for their participation in *A Day in the Life of China*, the children were allowed to keep the cameras. Here is a selection of some of the images captured by this young team of photographers.

Cong Xiaoling, Age 6, Chengdu, Sichuan

Zhao Jun, Age 13, Chengdu, Sichuan

Tang Lei, Age 6, Khotan, Xinjiang

Yuan Yi, Age 8, Beijing

Li Rui, Age 10, Lanzhou, Gansu

Ma Qing, Age 11, Jishishan, Gansu

Hu Yuheng, Age 9, Beijing

Cao Hong, Age 10, Changsha, Hunan

Han Rongxin, Age 8, Beijing

Shen Chunrong, Age 12, Beijing

Cao Beibei, Age 6, Beijing

He Zhao, Age 11, Beijing

● *Right*

Chapped cheeks: Since diapers are almost unknown in China, keeping small children clean is a common problem. Specially constructed trousers for toddlers, available everywhere, provide a neat solution.
Photographer:
Mary Ellen Mark, USA

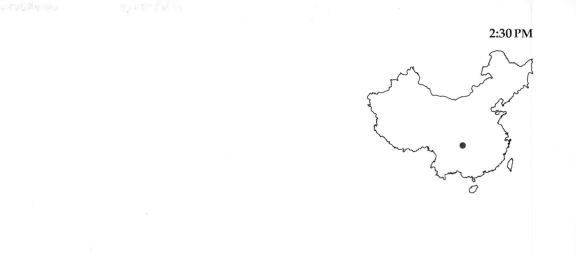

● *Above*

This Chinese teamster hauling toy tanks along Beijing's Chang'an Avenue must provide his own horsepower.
Photographer:
David Hume Kennerly, USA

● *Right*

April blizzards and yaks on Main Street are common sights in the Gansu city of Xiahe.
Photographer:
Dilip Mehta, Canada

● *Left*

Laundry day at a dormitory
for unmarried stevedores in
the port city of Haikou on
Hainan Island.
Photographer:
Torin Boyd, USA

● *Above*

Neither rain nor snow nor the
resulting slush and mud will
stay the men of Xiaohong from
their daily game of billiards.
Photographer:
Eric Lars Bakke, USA

● *Right*

Trouble right here in River City: In recent years, alarming numbers of pool and billiard tables have sprung up along roadsides all over China. In Jinghong, a small city on the Lancang River, even the Buddhist monks have succumbed.
Photographer:
Diego Goldberg, Argentina

● *Following page*

Bai-minority children in Yunnan shy away from cameras. So British photographer Barry Lewis played a game. "The kids would hide, then I'd go seek. After a few minutes we were having so much fun everyone forgot about the camera."
Photographer:
Barry Lewis, Great Britain

● *Above*

Based on his advertising, this Kashgar dentist should probably be avoided.
Photographer:
Bruno Barbey, France

● *Right*

Here in Hebei, anesthetic is a luxury few curbside dentists like Chen Shoushan can afford.
Photographer:
Andy Levin, USA

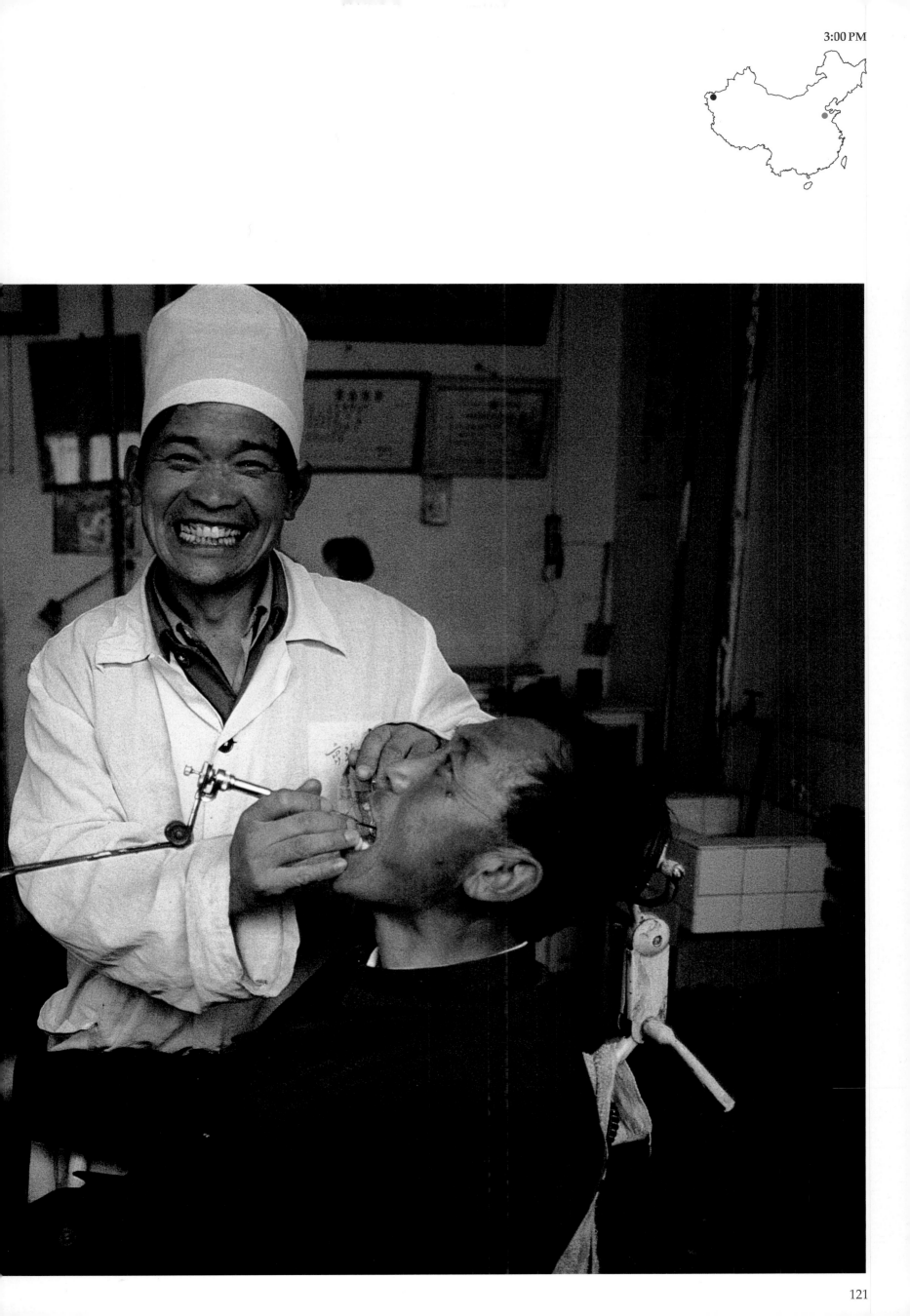

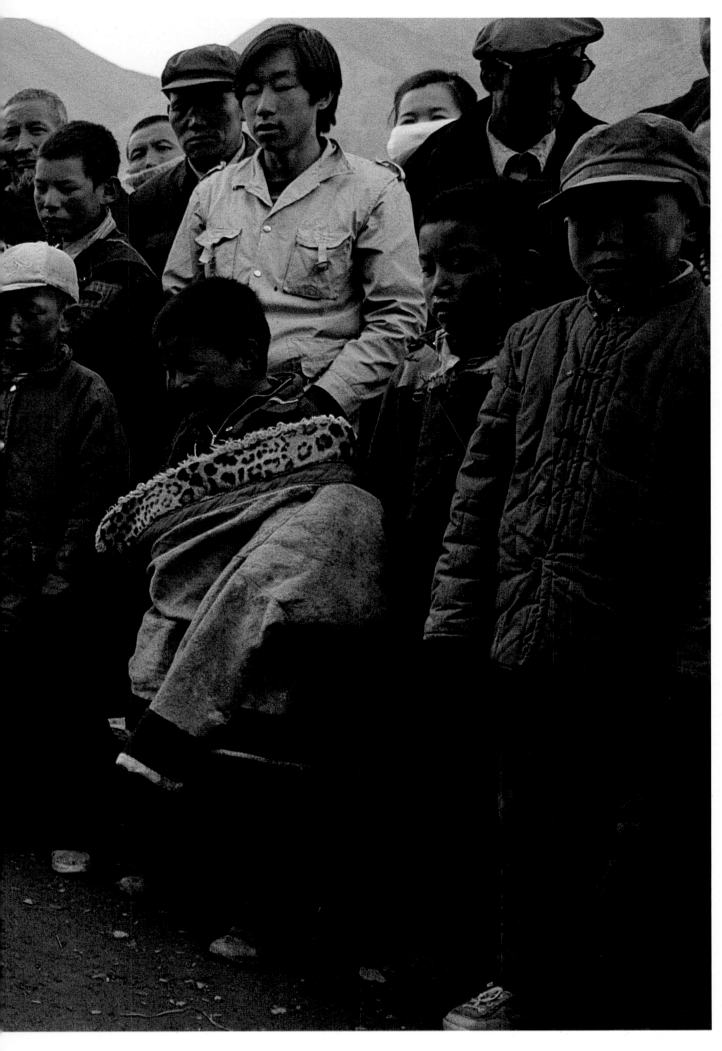

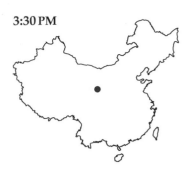

● *Left and previous pages 126-127*

Buddhist monasteries accept male novices at any age, but only a small number ever become ordained monks or lamas ("perfect teachers"). Most monks are responsible for secular jobs such as carpentry, accounting or road building, but all must assemble each fortnight to recite the rules of the *Vinaya*. These strict guidelines prohibit, among other things, theft, sexual intercourse and exaggeration of one's spiritual powers.

Many Buddhist temples destroyed during the Cultural Revolution have been rebuilt by the Chinese government. Still, the number of monks and their activities are closely monitored. Once there were 4,000 monks at the Labrang Tibetan Monastery in Gansu. Today, only 500 are allowed.
Photographer:
Dilip Mehta, Canada

● *Left*

The Baoshan General Iron and Steel Works in Shanghai is one of the most important enterprises in China. With state-of-the-art machinery from the West and employee wages averaging just $2 a day, it could become enormously profitable. Still, its future remains uncertain due to undependable supplies of coal and iron ore.
Photographer:
Sebastião Salgado, Brazil

• *Previous page 132*

A collier at the Chang Han Gou mine near Baotou, Inner Mongolia. Here, miners wield picks and shovels for eight hours at a time in dark, icy caverns 300 feet below the surface.
Photographer:
Nick Kelsh, USA

• *Previous page 133*

Baking unleavened bread in the Uighur city of Khotan is hot work. The baker reaches down into the fire pit and slaps dough on the red-hot oven wall. Minutes later, he retrieves a Frisbee-shaped *naan* which can be sold in the nearby market for 12 cents.
Photographer:
Jim Richardson, USA

• *Below*

For centuries, the women of Yunnan's isolated Naxi tribe enjoyed a matriarchal society. Men stayed home and did the cooking; women exercised domestic authority, inherited all property and complained when supper was late. Contact with the outside world, however, has led to a slow disintegration of the system.
Photographer:
Jodi Cobb, USA

• *Following page*

When Mao died and the Cultural Revolution ended, workers in Luoyang changed the name of their factory from the East Is Red Tractor Plant to Number One Tractor Plant. The color of the tractors remained the same.
Photographer:
Robin Moyer, USA

Nomadic families roaming the grasslands of Inner Mongolia measure their wealth not by the size of their homes, but by the number of carts needed to carry their food and belongings. In fact, their dwellings–called yurts–are all pretty much the same: heavy felt blankets draped over collapsible willow frames. In 1988, government bureaucrats introduced modern fiberglass yurts. The Mongols said no thanks. Willow and felt had served them well for the past few thousand years.
Photographer:
Yang Xiaolu, China

The Zhoushan Archipelago off the coast of Zhejiang is one of the richest fisheries in China. Fishing is prohibited during the April spawning season, however, so the men stay dockside, mending nets and spinning yarns.
Photographer:
Chen Changfen, China

At the Workers Sanitorium on Lake Tai, patients like Wang Yuxian prefer acupuncture to antibiotics. A fundamental component of Chinese medicine for more than 2,500 years, acupuncture seeks to correct the flow and distribution of energy, called *qi*, through channels, or meridians, inside the body. Though acupuncture is not completely understood, doctors theorize that the needles block certain nerve impulses. However it works, acupuncture has been proven an effective remedy for the pain of arthritis and rheumatism and can even be used in place of anesthesia during complicated operations.
Photographer:
Volker Hinz, W. Germany

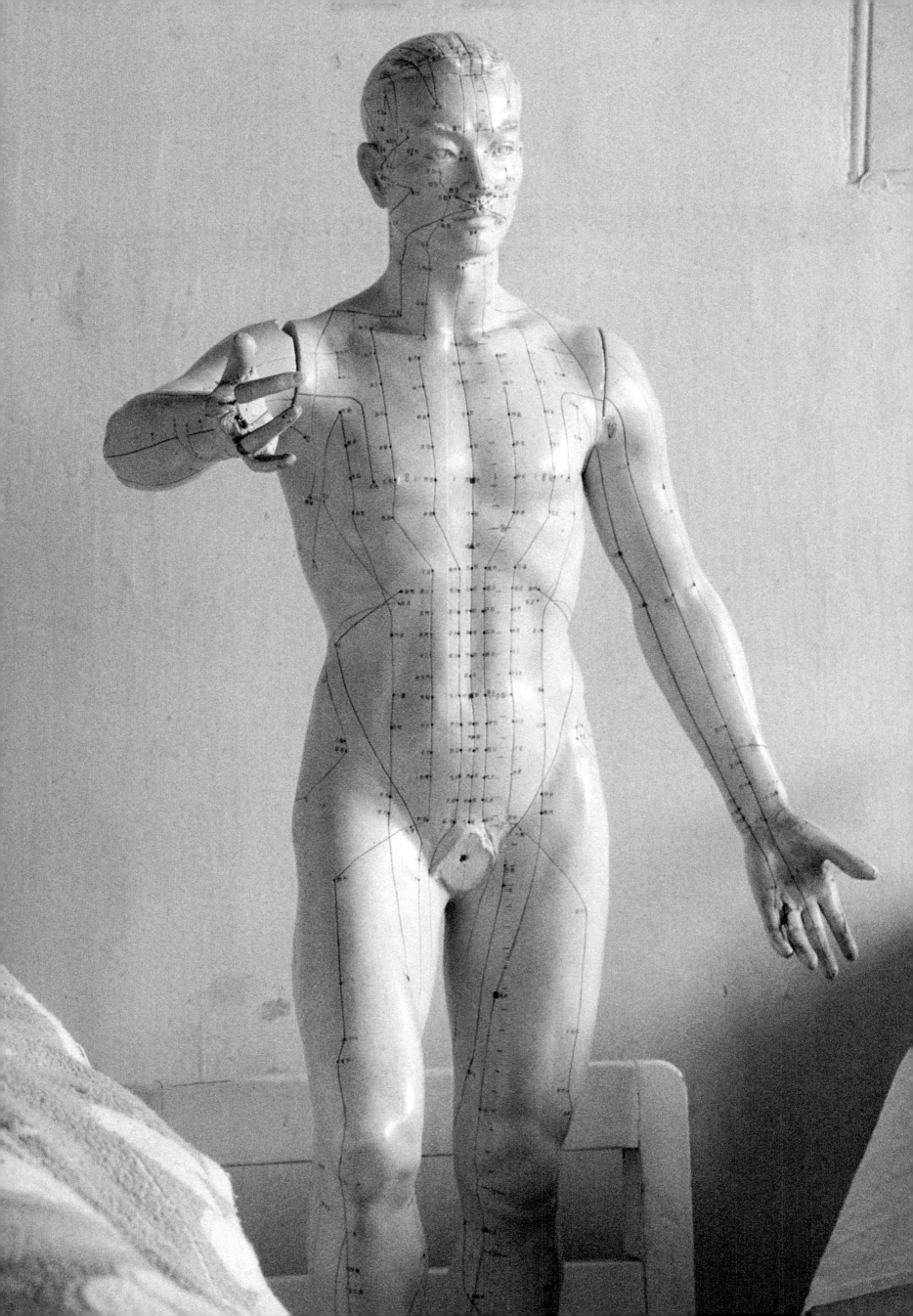

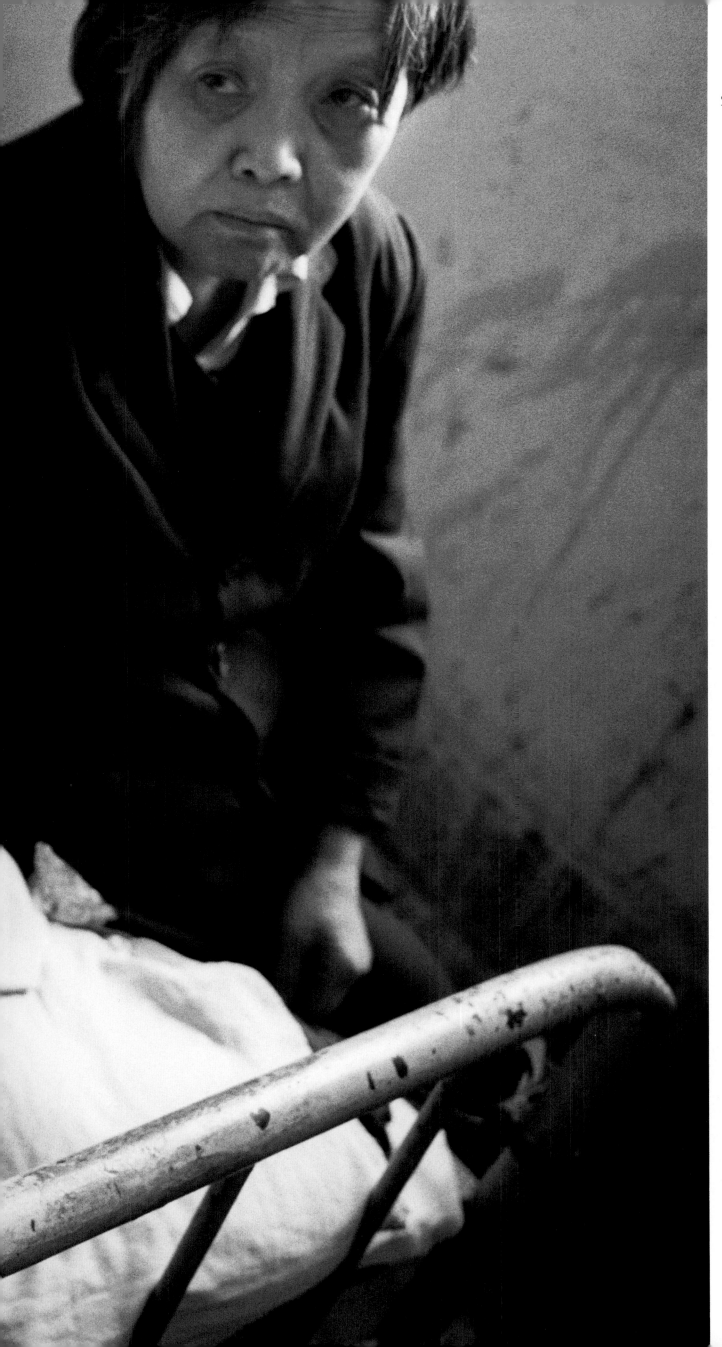

● *Left and following pages*

When photographer Mary Ellen Mark entered the Second Mental Hospital of Chongqing, she was prepared for the worst. Instead, she found a dedicated medical staff and 600 well-cared-for patients. Mark occasionally forgot that most of the people she photographed were suffering from psychosis.

As she accompanied doctors on their rounds, Mark found the staff very relaxed about patient behavior. "In the United States the emphasis is often on punishment, but here doctors seemed almost amused by the craziness. If someone was acting really psychotic, nurses and patients alike would laugh along. There seemed to be no underlying threat of punishment."

China's attitudes about mental health were not always so enlightened. As recently as the 19th century, many Chinese believed mental disorders resulted from demonic possession. During the Cultural Revolution, all mental facilities were closed and psychiatrists denounced for their "bourgeois" medical theories.

"It's impossible to take pictures that make a mental hospital look glamorous, but the atmosphere at Chongqing was actually very open," Mark says. "No one behaved as if they were ashamed. Shock therapy was openly discussed. The patients were allowed to act out their problems without being restrained."

"At the end of my stay I was beginning to relate to people's obsessions. They, in turn, had become very relaxed around me. As I was leaving, one very shy woman came up and said she loved me."
Photographer:
Mary Ellen Mark, USA

145

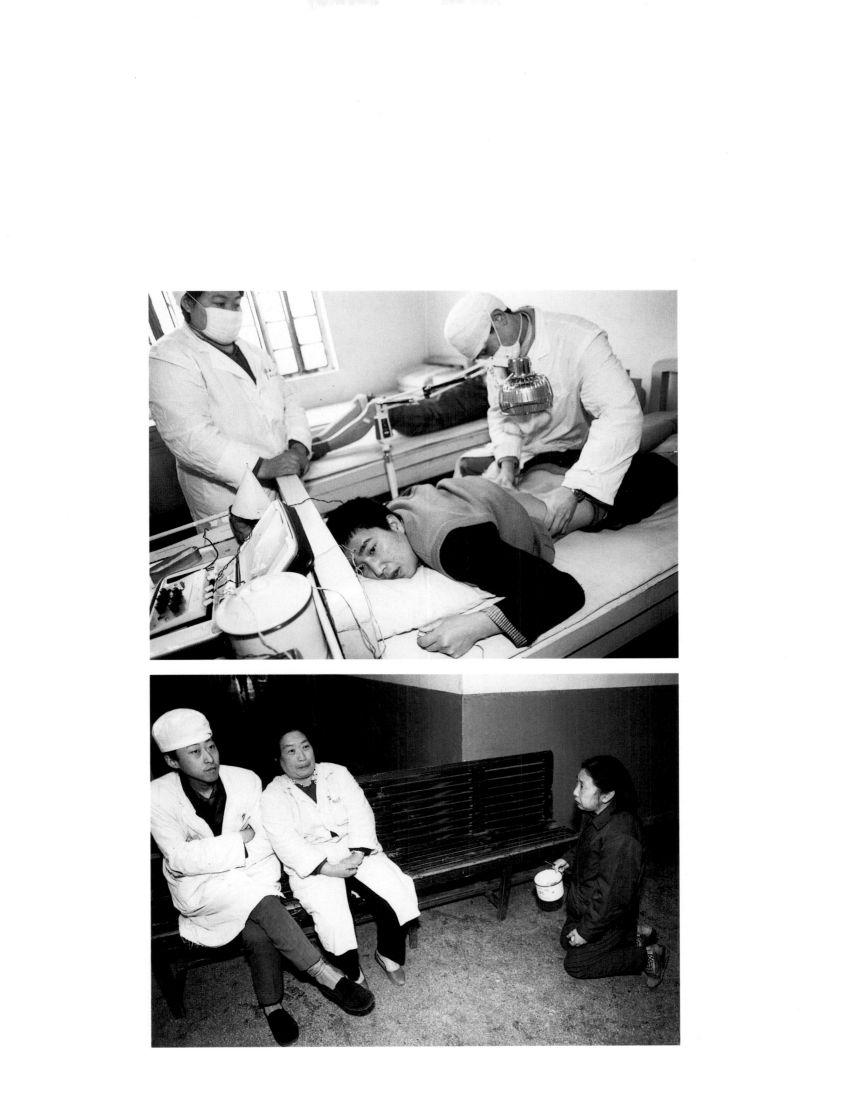

● *Right*

Horsing around: Before they marry, young Kazakh nomads play Catch the Maiden. The courting ritual begins with a pair of sweethearts on horse-back. The man gallops after his beloved in pursuit of a kiss. If and when he succeeds, the maiden becomes the pursuer, and tries to flail her beau with a riding crop. It's not a game for everyone, but on the high plains of Xinjiang where good horsemanship is essential, Catch the Maiden is a pragmatic test of a future spouse's riding ability.
Photographer:
Jay Dickman, USA

● *Left*

Much of China's revolutionary past has been discarded in the drive toward modernization. But survivors of the legendary Long March, like Wang Jun, 70 (pictured with his wife, Hou Zhuoping, 58), are still revered for their bravery.

Surrounded by the numerically superior Nationalist forces of Chiang Kai-shek, Communist troops led by Mao Zedong escaped from the mountains of Jiangxi Province in October 1934 and began a grueling 6,000-mile trek that ended 12 months later in Shaanxi. Of the 80,000 revolutionaries who began the march, only a few thousand survived to fight–and eventually win–the battle for China.
Photographer:
Peter Haley, USA

● *Above*

Nearly 23,000 marriages take place in China every day, but few are as colorful as this Bai-minority ceremony in Dali. One thousand years ago, the Bai Empire extended from Sichuan deep into Laos and Burma. But Bai troops were no match for the Mongol hordes of Kublai Khan, which overran the stronghold at Iron Armor Mountain in the 13th century. Though their ancient kingdom is only a memory and their numbers have shrunk to less than one million, the Bai culture still thrives. Even today, young Bai brides wear mirrors on their stomachs to deflect entreaties from demons.
Photographer:
Barry Lewis, Great Britain

● *Left*

In 1959, an ideological dispute between Mao Zedong and Nikita Khrushchev prompted a bitter rift between China and the Soviet Union. By that time, however, Anna Khuselina and other Russians living in the Mongolian city of Hailar had Chinese spouses, mixed-blood children and dozens of grand-children on the way. After 59 years in China, Khuselina, now 87, speaks excellent Chinese, but refuses to give up her ba-bushka. One month after this four-generation portrait was made, Beijing and Moscow normalized relations and each began withdrawing troops from the Sino-Soviet border 68 miles away.
Photographer:
Yang Xiaolu, China

● *Left*

When photographer Jay Dickman aimed his camera at Bahai, 12, and Xiabai, 8–two Kazakh kids playing on the Kongnesi Stud Farm in Xinjiang–Bahai jumped on his pony and galloped away. "Bahai didn't want his parents to find out he was smoking," Dickman said.

Photographer:
Jay Dickman, USA

● *Above*

Yongding County in Fujian is a major center for the cultivation of *yan cao* or "smoke weed." Prior to 1949, tobacco was considered an anti-malarial drug, and to insure that effect, a small amount of arsenic was added during the curing process. Today, cigarettes are enormously popular in China. More land is set aside for tobacco than for tea.

Photographer:
David Alan Harvey, USA

Puppy chow: For Cantonese
gourmands, man's best friend
can also be a delicious main
course. Plumped with white
rice for nine months, puppies
are said to yield a delightful
"fragrant meat" that alleviates
fatigue. Dark-colored pups
taste the best, say the Cantonese, but a white dog will do if
marinated properly. Cantonese
also eat cats, rodents and,
according to non-Cantonese,
"anything else with four legs
but the chairs they're sitting in."
Photographer:
Gerd Ludwig, W. Germany

● *Below*

Bereaved families in the village of Xiang Qian in Fujian show an extra measure of respect for the deceased by hiring a brass band to accompany the funeral procession.
Photographer:
Guy Le Querrec, France

● *Following page*

Hidajetulla Hoja, a Moslem missionary and saint, is buried at the Abakh Hoja Tomb in Kashgar. Seventy-two of his descendants lie beneath the conical burial mounds outside.
Photographer:
Bruno Barbey, France

● *Following pages 168-169*

On roads leading into the city of Khotan, rows of poplar trees provide protection from winds blowing off the Taklimakan Desert in western China.
Photographer:
Jim Richardson, USA

● *Left*

During the spring monsoon, commuting by bicycle along the rainy boulevards of Guangzhou is part of the daily grind.
Photographer:
Gerd Ludwig, W. Germany

Mid-afternoon at the Ningbo train station in Zhejiang.
Photographer:
Chen Changfen, China

Standing Room Only: China has one of the most extensive rail systems in the world. It also has the least expensive ticket prices. "You can travel one stop by train for the price of an egg, and all the way to Beijing for the price of a chicken," goes a popular saying. Since everyone can afford to take the train, however, seats sell rapidly, and those left with SRO tickets have to fight for space.
Photographer:
Li Binbin, China

● *Above*

The high demand for train tickets often forces travelers like this young couple transferring in Beijing to spend several days waiting for space to become available.
Photographer:
Paul Chesley, USA

● *Right*

Members of the Uighur minority, like this young man, dominate the huge Xinjiang Autonomous Region. They are among the few people who willingly traverse the Taklimakan Desert, a desolate region whose name in the Uighur language means "If you go in you won't come out."
Photographer:
Jim Richardson, USA

The Changbai Mountains in Jilin are blessed with some of China's last unpolluted hot springs. Olympic athletes on the national skiing and skating teams practice here. At the end of the day many of the athletes and their coaches soak their aching bodies in the soothing mineral waters.

Photographer:
Yang Dan, China

The days when Kazakh herdsmen can freely roam the steppes of wind-swept Xinjiang are rapidly drawing to a close. The first blow to their nomadic lifestyle came during the 1950s, when Mao divided the open plain into vast state farms. Then, in the 1970s, the government further subdivided the land, assigning parcels to homesteading Han Chinese. Today, little open rangeland remains.

Photographer:
Jay Dickman, USA

● *Above*

Horse sense: Scenic vistas along Guilin's Li River are seldom disturbed by modern bridges and highways. That pleases landscape artists, but it makes crossing the river more difficult.
Photographer:
Frans Lanting, Netherlands

● *Right*

By the end of the second century A.D., Chinese emperors had discarded their cherished Mongolian ponies in favor of hardier steeds like this one from Central Asia. One Han dynasty emperor believed these horses could transport him to heaven, and gave them the name *tian ma*, or heavenly horse. Today, *Ma*, or horse, is the most common surname in northwest China.
Photographer:
Jay Dickman, USA

● *Following page*

Homeward bound carrying the evening's water supply on the Liusha River, Yunnan.
Photographer:
Diego Goldberg, Argentina

● *Previous page*

In the mountain city of Dali, workers trudge home from local cement and paper mills. Pristine Lake Erhai and buildings of lustrous marble have made Dali famous for its beauty. In the newer industrial section of town, however, form follows function.
Photographer:
Barry Lewis, Great Britain

● *Above*

Luxuries that come with an improving economy make life more enjoyable for Duan Shouqin, an engineer with the Benxi Environmental Protection Bureau.
Photographer:
Che Fu, China

● *Right*

Officially, Deng Xiaoping serves as chairman of the Central Committee's Military Commission. In reality, he is China's maximum leader. A revolutionary strategist and diplomat, Deng survived the Long March and twice rebounded from political disgrace during the Cultural Revolution. For Deng, April 15th was like most other Saturday nights. He and his wife Zhuo Lin spent the evening babysitting their grandson.
Photographer:
Yang Shaoming, China

● *Following page*

Night falls on the island city of Xiamen off the coast of Fujian.
Photographer:
David Alan Harvey, USA

●*Left*

Even in Guangzhou–opened
to the West long before other
Chinese cities–public displays
of affection are rare and pre-
marital sex is strongly discour-
aged. This is due partially to
the historically puritanical
nature of Chinese society and
partially to the government's
population-control campaign.
Signs all over China say,
"Marry late. Have one child."
Photographer:
Gerd Ludwig, W. Germany

●*Above*

Sichuan teens zap alien centi-
pedes on a curbside video game
set up by a savvy entrepreneur
in the small town of Wuxi.
Photographer:
Rick Rickman, USA

●*Following page*

The Tashilhunpo Monastery in
Xigaze, Tibet, has been a center
for the study of Tantric Buddhism since the 15th century.
Like Mahayana Buddhism,
which is practiced elsewhere in
China, the Tantric sect preaches
the concepts of reincarnation
and nirvana (the state at which
the soul is finally released from
mortal existence). Tantric Bud-
dhists, however, believe that
through vigorous study and
meditation, they can bypass
reincarnation and reach
nirvana in a single lifetime.
Photographer:
Steve McCurry, USA

●*Following pages 196-197*

The Liang Family operates a
restaurant in Guangzhou's
Qingping market. After the
dinner rush is over, they play
cards and watch television.
Photographer:
Gerd Ludwig, W. Germany

● *Left*

When these old friends in the Fujian town of Hukeng get together, it's usually around steaming cups of tea. The Chinese speak glowingly of a tea's "character," much like the French praise wine. In the *Chinese Book of Tea*, published in the eighth century, author Lu Yu wrote, "Tea may shrink and crackle like a Mongol's boot. Or it may look like the dewlap of a wild ox. . . . It can look like a mushroom in whirling flight just as clouds do when they float out from behind a mountain peak."
Photographer:
David Alan Harvey, USA

● *Following page*

Cormorant fishing is based on centuries-old principles: Cormorants are afraid of the dark, so they stay close to the lantern placed at the bow of their master's fishing punt. Hempen cords around their necks prevent them from swallowing the fish they catch. Once their throats are full, the birds jump aboard and disgorge their prize. Fisherman Hong Yinchang gives his birds small fish every so often to keep them motivated.
Photographer:
Frans Lanting, Netherlands

● *Right*

On the island of Qingbin in the
East China Sea, fishing
families crowd the local meet-
ing hall to catch the latest
attraction: a troupe of traveling
magicians and acrobats. Many
itinerant performers are recent
high-school graduates who
leave tedious, government-
assigned jobs in the city to take
their show on the road.
Typically, the players exhibit
more enthusiasm than finesse,
but on tiny Qingbin this agile
19 year old still packs them in.
Photographer:
Chen Changfen, China

● *Following page*

In the village of Xiniujiao, the
work day begins at 10 p.m.
when deep-ocean fishermen
make ready to sail. Most of
these men of the sea were born
and raised on fishing junks
and rarely set foot in the
village itself. So accustomed
are they to the ebb and flow of
life on the water that those
who do venture ashore often
become "land sick."
Photographer:
Claus C. Meyer, W. Germany

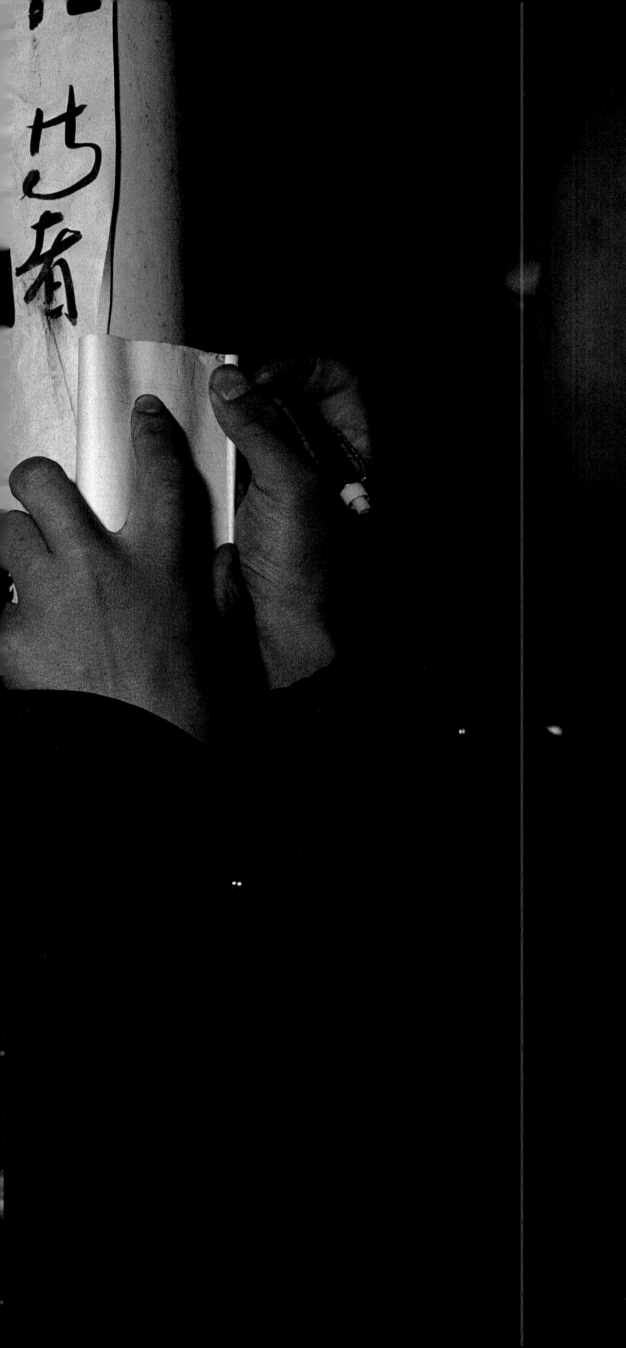

● *Left*

"All Beijing University mourns!
See who prospers, who despairs.
In 40 years, China has failed
*   to rise.*
In 70 years, democracy remains
*   unfulfilled.*
Deng Xiaoping still has his
*   health at 84.*
Hu Yaobang dies first at 73.
The politicians come and go.
Can there be no cure?"

As *A Day in the Life of China* wound to a close, a small spark of protest was lit at Beijing University. It would soon explode into a full-blown conflagration.

Just before midnight, big-character posters commemorating the death of ousted liberal General Secretary Hu Yaobang began appearing on campus. Within two weeks, a million students, workers and professionals were occupying Tiananmen Square. Later, units of the People's Liberation Army would move onto the Square, resulting in the tragic loss of many lives. A profound political, military and social struggle ensued.

It seemed clear that 40 years after the founding of the People's Republic and thousands of years after the dawn of the first dynasty, China was still changing, still growing and still struggling to reach its awesome potential.
Photographer:
Anonymous

人民共和国万岁

Photographers' Assignment Locations

Paul Christopher Sancya, Jiuquan

On April 15, 1989 photographers from around the world traveled on Northwest Airlines to join their Chinese counterparts in Beijing for *A Day in the Life of China*. Our special thanks to Northwest Airlines. Their experience flying to Asia ensured the success of this unique venture.

1 Abbas	31 Huang Jingzheng	61 Graeme Outerbridge
2 Eric Lars Bakke	32 Nick Kelsh	62 Bill Pierce
3 Bruno Barbey	33 David Hume Kennerly	63 Larry C. Price
4 Nicole Bengiveno	34 Douglas Kirkland	64 Eli Reed
5 Bi Qiang	35 Steve Krongard	65 Roger Ressmeyer
6 Torin Boyd	36 Jean-Pierre Laffont	66 Jim Richardson
7 Marilyn Bridges	37 Frans Lanting	67 Rick Rickman
8 Michael Bryant	38 Sarah Leen	68 Joe Rossi
9 René Burri	39 Guy Le Querrec	69 Sebastião Salgado
10 Che Fu	40 Andy Levin	70 Paul Christopher Sancya
11 Chen Changfen	41 Barry Lewis	71 George Steinmetz
12 Paul Chesley	42 Li Binbin	72 Patrick Tehan
13 Ed Cismondi, Sr.	43 Li Qianguang	73 Neal Ulevich
14 Bradley Clift	44 Li Weishun	74 Jerry Valente
15 Jodi Cobb	45 Liu Tiesheng	75 Wang Miao
16 Don Cochran	46 John Loengard	76 Wang Wenlan
17 Dai Shunqing	47 Long Yunhe	77 Dan White
18 Jay Dickman	48 Gerd Ludwig	78 Wu Jinsheng
19 Misha Erwitt	49 Ma Zengyin	79 Wu Shouzhuang
20 Gerrit Fokkema	50 Ma Zhongyuan	80 Wu Zhiyi
21 Raphaël Gaillarde	51 Mary Ellen Mark	81 Xu Zhigang
22 Gao Bo	52 Stephanie Maze	82 Yang Changzhong
23 Sam Garcia	53 Steve McCurry	83 Yang Dan
24 John Giannini	54 Wally McNamee	84 Yang Shaoming
25 Diego Goldberg	55 Dilip Mehta	85 Yang Xiaolu
26 Judy Griesedieck	56 Jim Mendenhall	86 Yuan Xuejun
27 Peter Haley	57 Doug Menuez	87 Zhang Tongsheng
28 David Alan Harvey	58 Claus C. Meyer	88 Zhao Zhonglu
29 He Yanguang	59 Robin Moyer	89 Zhou Yi
30 Volker Hinz	60 Randy Olson	90 Zhu Xianmin

XINJIANG

QINGHAI

TIBET

Jean-Pierre Laffont, Boyang

Douglas Kirkland, Beijing

Nicole Bengiveno, Harbin

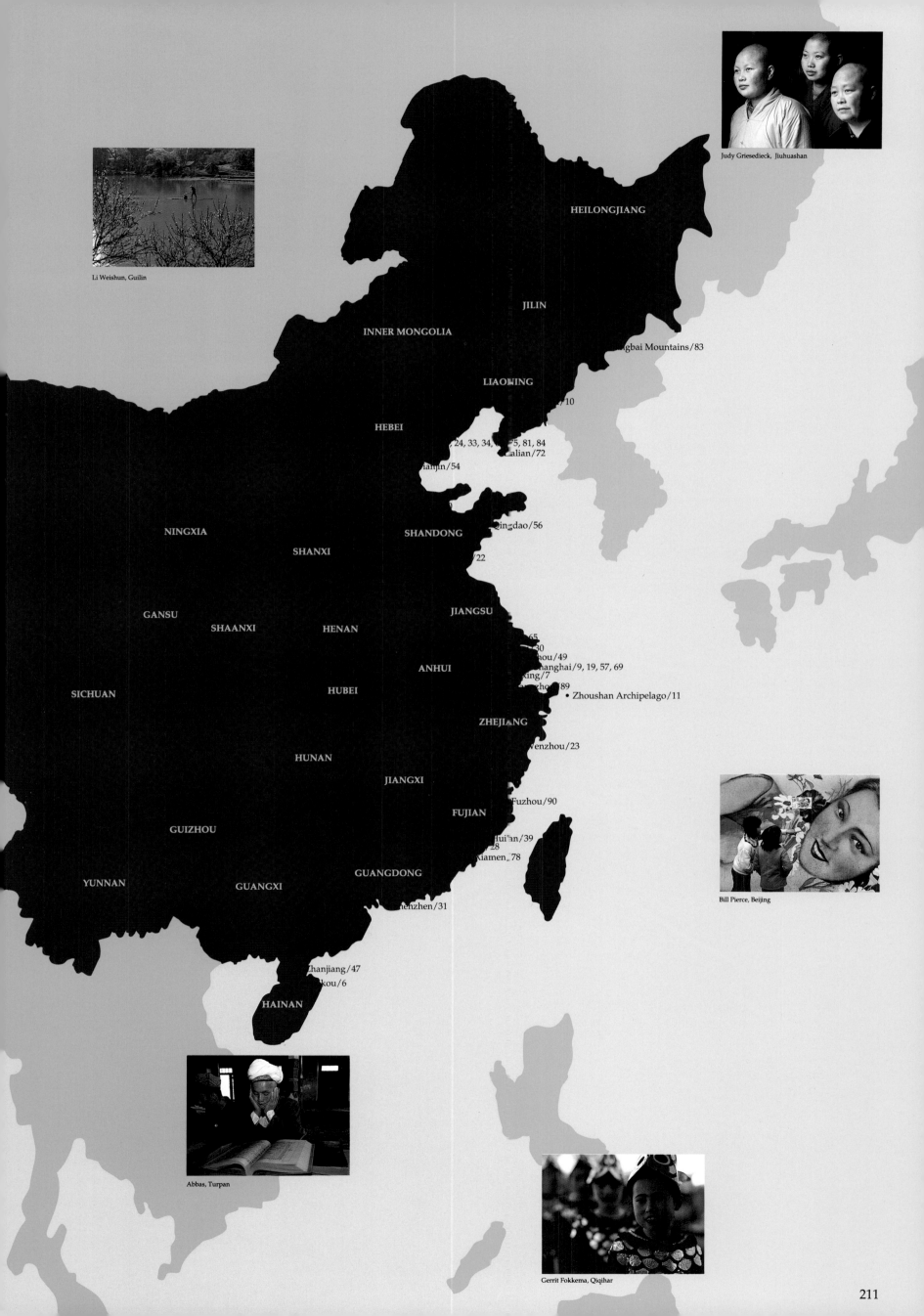

Judy Griesedieck, Jiuhuashan

Li Weishun, Guilin

HEILONGJIANG

JILIN

ngbai Mountains/83

INNER MONGOLIA

LIAONING

/10

HEBEI

24, 33, 34, 5, 81, 84
alian/72

iamn/54

NINGXIA

ingdao/56

SHANDONG

SHANXI

/22

GANSU

SHAANXI

HENAN

JIANGSU

65

ou/49
hanghai/9, 19, 57, 69
 king/7
zhou 89
• Zhoushan Archipelago/11

ANHUI

SICHUAN

HUBEI

ZHEJIANG

Wenzhou/23

HUNAN

JIANGXI

Fuzhou/90

FUJIAN

GUIZHOU

uian/39
28
Xiamen 78

YUNNAN

GUANGXI

GUANGDONG

henzhen/31

Bill Pierce, Beijing

Zhanjiang/47
kou/6

HAINAN

Abbas, Turpan

Gerrit Fokkema, Qiqihar

211

2. Bi Qiang

3. Linda Lamb

2. Harbin-ger: On assignment in the Heilonjiang city of Harbin, *New York Daily News* photographer Nicole Bengiveno hunts for a better angle.
3. Gang of three: Assignment Editor Bill Messing, Managing Editor Mark Rykoff and General Manager Jennifer Erwitt enjoy a brief moment of relaxation.
4. Eastern exposure: Project Director David Cohen is just one of the comrades with the Chinese photographers.
5. Swing Lo: CNPITC President Lou Ming, Interpreter Wang Juan and Production Coordinator Kate Yuschenkoff savor the taste of Mao Tai at a traditional Chinese banquet.

5. Jennifer Erwitt

4. Roger Ressmeyer

1. Abbas/Magnum

The Day in the Life of China you have just experienced began much like any other. Atop Mt. Emei, Buddhist pilgrims rose with the dawn and began their search for sacred rainbows. A fresh wind kept fishermen in the Zhoushan Archipelago close to port. From Shandong in the north to Guangdong in the south, the last day of China's work week started, as it does every Saturday, precisely at 8 a.m.

This day–April 15, 1989–was different from most days, however. Nearly 100 of the world's finest photojournalists from five continents were positioned throughout the country in every province and autonomous region. Their assignment: to make remarkable pictures of everyday life; to record an ancient country in the midst of mind-boggling social and economic change. Between them, they would shoot 140,000 frames of film in a single day. The results would be gathered in a book to be published on the 40th anniversary of the founding of the People's Republic of China.

But April 15 would be an extraordinary day even without the intervention of the world's finest photojournalists. For while the photographers were setting out on assignment just before dawn, former Communist Party General Secretary Hu Yaobang breathed his last. Hu had been removed from office two years earlier, and in the intervening years many Chinese had come to identify him with personal liberty and free speech.

As shutters clicked and motor drives whirred, news of Hu's death spread across the country and public disorder seldom seen in a socialist state slowly began to build. By the evening of April 15, anti-government posters were springing up on the campus of Beijing University. By midnight, there were flowers and placards on the Monument to the People's Heroes in Tiananmen Square. The turmoil had begun.

The *Day in the Life* photographers–sensitive to the stirrings of a Big Story–soon realized that the repercussions of their day in China might last several months, if not longer. They were witnessing a political upheaval, its duration and direction unknown. Before it was over, there would be countless dead and wounded. Many decided to stay and see the thing through.

By April 18, Magnum photographer Abbas was spending long hours covering demonstrations in Beijing. As the hours passed and the crowds grew to over 100,000, he was joined by *US News & World Report*'s Bill Pierce and Judy Griesedieck of the *San Jose Mercury News*. Robin Moyer of *Time* flew back to Beijing from Hong Kong and was present in Beijing when the occupation of Tiananmen Square came to an end.

It was clear that the *Day in the Life* team had once again arrived at a crucial point in time. It was sort of uncanny. In 1985, *A Day in the Life of Japan* was among the first photography books to acknowledge capitalism's newest champ. In 1986, the publication of *A Day in the Life of America* followed shortly after the Statue of Liberty celebrations–the high-water mark of Reaganism and American pride. In 1987, Collins' portrait of the Soviet Union coincided with the first blush of *glasnost* and the rise of Gorbachev.

For *Day in the Life* Editor David Cohen, the timing of the China project seemed to arise from a combination of general trends and plain chance. "The world's most populous superpower is also its most rapidly changing country," he said. "But we had no idea that the changes would kick off so explosively."

Preparations for *A Day in the Life of China* began in the spring of 1988 when Collins Publishers was approached by John Owen of Weldon Owen Publishing in Hong Kong. For years, both companies had wanted to publish a definitive portrait of China. By pooling their resources, each could achieve its goal. Cohen had negotiated Days in the Life in eight other countries, including the Soviet Union. But two quick trips to China soon convinced him that lessons learned with one communist superpower did not necessarily apply to the other.

"Soviet officials bargained hard, but once they finally said yes, you knew you had a deal," Cohen explained. "In China, the officials said yes to many things, but you never knew what would actually happen. The boss may say go while the cadre says no. The first thing we learned was never take yes for an answer."

Cohen needed help from local partners with publishing experience and Chinese political savvy. With guidance from Weldon Owen and a consulting firm founded by Stephen FitzGerald, the former Australian ambassador to China, Cohen found a collaborator in the person of Lou Ming, president of the China National Publishing Industry Trading Corporation (CNPITC). A former Chinese diplomat in Africa, Lou was comfortable with foreigners–his company was publishing a book about George Bush–and experienced in the intricacies of Chinese bureaucracies. Cohen's team became complete with the addition of Lin Tingsong and Zhou Wanping, director and vice-director of the Great Wall Publishing House. As the publishing wing of the People's Liberation Army, Great Wall had the logistical capability to send photographers to the farthest corners of China and assure cooperation when they got there. Normally, the two organizations were fierce competitors. But John Owen had brought them together before, and the prospect of being associated with a prestigious project turned them into temporary colleagues.

Even with this sort of assistance, many of the old China hands slumped about the oval-shaped bar at the Foreign Correspondents' Club in Hong Kong doubted the project would ever get off the ground. Their cynicism was not unfounded. Though equal in size to the United States, China had one-eighth the roads–most of them better suited to horse carts than cars. Its national airline, CAAC, had an enormous fleet, but its flights were routinely and inexplicably cancelled or delayed. The chances of all the photographers arriving at their assigned locations on April 15 and then getting back in time to drop their film were minuscule, said the sages. A few began to talk about MIAs.

These daunting administrative headaches didn't dampen enthusiasm on the other side of the Pacific. Unworried about the potential logistical nightmares, photographers by the hundreds began applying for *DITLOC* positions. During February 1989 alone more than 250 applications arrived. Hoping to better his chances, one aspirant even sent rice and chopsticks along with his portfolio.

During the early weeks of 1989, however, the first priority was to recruit an administrative staff. For managing editor, Cohen selected Mark Rykoff, a specialist in Russian Studies from Columbia University's Harriman Institute who served as an assignment editor on *A Day in the Life of the Soviet Union*. Aided by Assistant Managing Editor David Spitzler, Rykoff went in search of assignment editors

7. Linda Lamb

8. Jennifer Erwitt

10. Linda Lamb

9. Michael Downey

6. Project photographers George Steinmetz, Paul Chesley and Frans Lanting pose with the Director and Vice Director of the Great Wall Publishing House, Lin Tingsong and Zhou Wanping.
7. Sino the times: Assignment Editor Martha Avery and Chinese Project Director Wei Mingxiang contemplate the success of the project.

familiar with China. In Bill Messing, a 28-year-old Dartmouth sinologist, and Martha Avery, a Wharton MBA living in Hong Kong, he found editors whose youth masked a total of 28 years of experience in China. Both were fluent in written and spoken Chinese and willing to devote the hours necessary to develop 360 specific photo assignments in 77 different locations.

Equally essential to the project's success was securing adequate corporate sponsorship. Toward this end, Collins' Corporate Relations Director Cathy Quealy began spending long days on the telephone. Raymond DeMoulin, director of Eastman Kodak's Professional Photography Division, was the first to offer financial assistance, along with 5,000 rolls of film and processing worth $120,000. Nikon and Bank of America agreed to help with additional financing; Federal Express, with shipping. Northwest Airlines came through with tickets that allowed photographers to travel to and from Asia.

For Travel Director Kate Kelly, the search for 1000 nights' worth of hotel rooms in Beijing and Hong Kong–cities with the highest hotel occupancy rates in Asia–ended when Holiday Inn offered to provide the necessary space. Getting the photographers back from remote places like Nanchang and Qiqihar remained a more vexing problem. Domestically, CAAC sold only one-way tickets, and it was usually impossible to buy them until three days before the flight. Enter Ke Weimin, a CNPITC staffer with the auspicious title of secretary to harmonize and book tickets and propagandize. Ke solved the transport problem by sending advance personnel to nearly every assigned location to book the necessary return tickets.

The state-controlled press posed no problems for *Day in the Life* Publicity Director Patti Richards. "The government was on our side, and we were actually able to order up a front-page story in the *People's Daily* that would reach millions of people the next day. This was an interesting change for an American publicist," she confided.

Six weeks prior to shoot day, files containing months of research, ten Macintosh computers on loan from Apple Hong Kong, assorted discs and printers plus an obstinate photocopying machine were sent via Federal Express to Beijing. There, they were escorted through the intricate Chinese customs bureaucracy by on-site Coordinator Harold Weldon.

8. Beijing connection: Two phone lines and ninety anxious photographers leave Interpreter Qiao Hong without a spare minute.
9. Patience and diplomacy make Sponsorship Director Cathy Quealy an excellent fund-raiser.
10. PRC PR: Chinese Photographer Li Weishun sees Publicity Director Patti Richards off at the airport.
11. Aussie-fied: China hand and Sydney native Harold Weldon pauses for a portrait session with a PLA tourist at the Great Wall.
12. The Collins staff on the terrace of their San Francisco offices.

11. Mark Rykoff

12. Doug Menuez

The shipment coincided with the arrival of 1,900 pounds of film, T-shirts, backpacks and stationery from Logistics Coordinator Jim Kordis and Production Assistant Monica Baltz in San Francisco. From that point on, it was up to Office Manager Linda Lamb and Production Coordinator Kate Yuschenkoff to transform the Holiday Inn Lido's Marco Ballroom into a state-of-the-art computer facility. The two soon discovered that making 220-volt monitors compatible with 110-volt disc drives would not be easy, especially in a country where plugs and sockets are not uniform. "We had to rewire everything," remembers Yuschenkoff. "We became electrical contractors overnight."

The computers eventually blinked to life; the issue of Daylight Savings Time took longer to resolve. "We asked five different people at CAAC and received five different answers," smiles *Day in the Life*'s General Manager Jennifer Erwitt. "Our interest was more than academic, since by that time our flight schedule was so tightly coordinated that an hour's difference either way would have caused dozens of people to miss their flights."

For Qiao Hong, the conscientious interpreter on loan from CNPITC, Erwitt's passion for organization was a source of continuing amazement. "My impression of your country was mistaken because I used to escort American lawyers," he admitted during a moment of candor. "They only were interested in luxury, and I could never imagine them doing hard work. But that small girl Jennifer won't stop working until everything is in order."

On the evening of Monday, April 10, two days before they dispersed to more than 77 destinations in China, *DITLOC* photographers gathered in Beijing for a round of feasting, Chinese style. At a dinner hosted by Nikon, Zhou Wanping introduced them to the subtleties of Great Wall wine and the infamously potent Mao Tai liquor, a fire-and-ice combination whose synergistic effect was felt long into the following afternoon.

The prospect of a second high-octane banquet at the Great Hall of the People on April 11 did not diminish the enthusiasm at an afternoon Childrens' Photo Workshop organized with the help of Kodak's China Branch Manager, Frances Lee, at the Working People's Cultural Palace.

"For professional photographers a *Day in the Life* project is a wonderful vacation," laughed Sygma Photo Agency cofounder Jean-Pierre Laffont, who was forced to spend a *Day in the Life of Japan* taking photos from a wheelchair. "We share rooms and ideas, then go out and compete with all the energy we can muster."

By Wednesday morning, however, the bonhomie of the previous evening was wearing thin as anxious photographers waited to see if their flights would leave. "I'm always scared before I start to photograph a story," said former *Life* magazine Photo Editor John Loengard, nervously pacing the Lido lobby. "The worrying continues until I've taken my first good picture. For me, that photograph is like the violinist's 'A,' the key on which all the other players in an orchestra tune. Until I get that key-note picture, it's difficult for me to be very socially agreeable."

Ideally, the schedule arranged by the Chinese project directors —Great Wall's Wei Mingxiang and CNPITC's Chang Zhenguo— would give every photographer at least one day and possibly two to reconnoiter prior to shoot day on Saturday. Michael Bryant's trip to Sichuan's remote Jiuzhaigou Valley, though, ended at inhospitable Pingwu after his all-terrain jeep bogged down in muck. "There was an alternate path leading up into the mist, but the driver blanched at my suggestion we follow it," remembers the *Philadelphia Inquirer* staff photographer. "Many snows, many snows," he said. "I argued the point, of course, until he mentioned that an avalanche the day before had buried a tour bus, killing two passengers."

For Pulitzer Prize-winner Dan White, Friday night arrived with the promise of an even better tomorrow. "There I was as the sun went down on this vast grassland in Inner Mongolia," he wistfully recalled, "I'm having refreshments with a wonderful family, experiencing the kind of hospitality that doesn't exist in America anymore."

On the summit of Mt. Emei April 15 dawned crisp and cold. For Graeme Outerbridge, whose assignment to cover Buddhist pilgrims read like a page from Chaucer's *Canterbury Tales*, the day actually had begun several hours earlier when he set up a time exposure with a 15mm lens, trying to streak the stars that glimmered in the false indigo dawn.

Two thousand miles to the west on the high plain of Xinjiang, Jay Dickman, another Pulitzer Prize-winner, was also on the move, trying to outdistance a salivating cur that belonged to nomadic Kazakhs. He lost the race. "I sluiced out the fang marks with water, painted my calf with antiseptic and went looking for a veterinarian," he grimaced.

After limping through clusters of tent-like structures known as yurts, Dickman at last found the doctor, who was busy castrating a horse. "The horse put up a fight, but in the end they tied him down and did the deed," Dickman sighs. "Standing there, waiting for my mouth to foam, I felt great empathy for that creature."

For most photographers, the frustrations encountered on April 15 were more prosaic. Zealous government guides prohibited pictures of a nude modeling studio in Chongqing, a hill tribe folk doctor in Yunnan and a rickshaw puller in Changsha. "When I pointed my camera at a beggar in Dali, a local man literally threw himself across my path," recalls Britain's Barry Lewis. "His line was that if the picture ever appeared in the book, there would be trouble. He was very frank and this time his candor worked: I didn't take the picture."

13. Gao Bo

16. Manuel J. Rodriguez

14. Chen Changfen

13. Flashback: An old Mengyin woman's collection of Mao pins reminds Chinese photographer Gao Bo of another era.
14. Camera crew: The children at the Kodak camera workshop get a chance to try out their brand-new cameras.
15. Piercing eye: Bill Pierce, of *US News and World Report*, gives an aspiring young photographer a few pointers.
16. Hotshot: Schoolchildren on their way to the flag-raising ceremony on Tiananmen Square draw the lens of former White House photographer David Hume Kennerly.

15. Manuel J. Rodriguez

17. Andy Levin

18. Doug Menuez

19. Mark Rykoff

17. Juggling assignments: Andy Levin gives a young Wuqiao acrobat a lift.
18. Hold the mayo: Steve McCurry tries to sort out some last minute details on a phone outside the Great Hall of the People.
19. On a roll: Kate Kelly instructs photographer Gerd Ludwig in the ancient art of numbering and labeling of film.

20. Eye sore: The *Day in the Life of China* picture editors gather after a long week at the light tables. They are (clockwise from lower left): Michele McNally of *Fortune*, Project Director David Cohen, Dieter Steiner of *Stern*, Alfonso Gutiérrez Escera, Art Director Jenny Barry, Michele Stephenson of *Time*, Sandra Eisert of the *San Jose Mercury News*, George Wedding of the *Sacramento Bee* and Peter Howe of *Life*. In the middle are Susan Vermazen of *New York* magazine and Eliane Laffont.

20. Dana Fineman

Chinese photographers seldom took no for an answer. After being ejected from a hospital for the criminally insane by cautious officials in Jinhua, He Yanguang of *China Youth News* telephoned contacts back in Beijing, then returned to the hospital and waited calmly until the action of provincial authorities was reversed.

The only *DITLOC* photographer to encounter serious danger was Li Weishun, a staff photographer for the Great Wall Publishing House sent to Friendship Pass on the Sino-Vietnamese border. A graduate of China's Naval Submarine Institute, Li ventured forth with a group of army engineers only to find himself in a mine field that had claimed the lives of two Chinese traders just that morning. "I went back to the base and left the exposed film shot earlier in the day in a safe place," Li later recalled. "I didn't want it to be destroyed if I stepped on a mine. Then I returned to continue photographing the engineers."

News photographers have a way of demanding more than they actually expect. In the case of former White House photographer David Hume Kennerly, requesting the impossible is standard operating procedure. On the morning of April 15 Kennerly asked his young interpreter to secure access to the roof of the Meridian Gate inside the Forbidden City. Told it was a prohibited area not even employees could enter, Kennerly responded, "Just explain that I'm the guy who photographed Zhou Enlai back in 1972. If Zhou were still here, he'd want me on top of that gate."

Assigned to photograph Tiananmen Square, Kennerly resigned himself to shooting the Forbidden City at ground level and went on to other things. At 3 p.m., however, his interpreter returned with a nervous Forbidden City groundskeeper who had a key ring that looked as if it was forged during the Ming dynasty. "I have used personal relationships with my cousin to unlock the door," she beamed with justifiable pride.

Once past a massive door whose hinges creaked from disuse, the three climbed a cobbled stairway to a narrow battlement last patrolled decades before by palace guards. Shards of Ming pottery were strewn along the path. "We ran hunched over along the wall, the entire Forbidden City before us," Kennerly remembers. "My guide was giggling; the groundskeeper was moaning. I looked through the viewfinder at a picture never before taken by an American journalist and thought, 'This is great.'"

For Jay Dickman, April 15 ended with a traditional Kazakh dinner attended by the apologetic owners of the dog. "The rice and meat were specially prepared, and presented along with assurances that the dog was not rabid. Only after chewing for 20 minutes did I finally ask what the meat was," Dickman remembers. "'Horse,' came the response. For the rest of the meal I felt as if I were eating Mr. Ed."

For Dickman and the rest of the *Day in the Life* photographers, the stroke of midnight on the 15th meant it was time to pack up their gear and head back to Beijing, where they would drop their film and catch flights to their next assignments all over the world. For them, the challenge was over. But for the *Day in the Life* staffers, a new challenge was just beginning. Getting the book published by October 1, in time for the 40th anniversary of the founding of the People's Republic would require that the editing, the layout and the caption-writing be completed in six weeks—half the time normally required to complete a *Day in the Life* book. An extraordinary effort ensued. The film was processed in record time by San Francisco's New Lab. Nine picture editors, from some of the world's top magazines and newspapers, worked around the clock for six straight days to reduce 140,000 frames of film to 400 "final selects." In a few short days, Art Director Jenny Barry, assisted by Charles Tyrone, sculpted these images into the 122 layouts that comprise the book. Production Director Stephanie Sherman logged many all-nighters at printer Dai Nippon to make sure that the photographs would not lose their luster in the book's final phase. Miraculously, everyone met their deadline and *A Day in the Life of China* went to press in time to be out in the fall.

A Day in the Life of China. A great adventure. A major story. Inadvertently, the record of an important day in recent Chinese history. For photojournalists who experienced April 15, and for the reader who has just relived it, this visual odyssey through China's cities and across its dusty plains is a portrait of a country that, in many respects, is still in the midst of tumultuous change. Forty years ago, on October 1, 1949, Mao Zedong founded the People's Republic of China. Standing atop the Gate of Heavenly Peace, he looked out on the multitude that filled Tiananmen Square and declared, "The Chinese people have now stood up." The question now is, "Where are they headed?"

—David DeVoss

Postscript:

As A Day in the Life of China *went to press, it became the subject of a growing controversy. Two of our associate publishers, the China National Publishing Industry Trading Corporation and the Great Wall Publishing House objected to the inclusion of certain photographs and some of the text in this book. Specifically, they requested the exclusion of the photographs which appear on pages 122-123 and 208-209. They further objected to any mention of the student democracy movement and the events which occurred in Tiananmen Square on June 3, 1989. Collins respectfully declined to make these changes, but agreed to print the disclaimer which appears on the title page of this book.*

Photographers' Biographies

Abbas
Iranian/Paris
An Iranian transplanted to the West, Abbas has covered major political events in Asia, Africa, the Middle East and Latin America. A member of Magnum photo agency, his work has appeared in most leading magazines over the past 20 years. Most recently, he has concentrated on depicting the role of Islam throughout the world.

Eric Lars Bakke
American/Denver, Colorado
A member of the Picture Group agency, Bakke received an honorable mention for a news picture story at the 1985 Pictures of the Year competition, sponsored by the National Press Photographers Association and held at the University of Missouri School of Journalism. A former chief photographer for the *Denver Post*, he now contributes regularly to numerous US news and feature magazines.

Bruno Barbey
French/Paris
A member of Magnum photo agency since 1966, Barbey has covered stories on every continent, and his work is regularly published in *Life*, the *Sunday Times* (London), *Stern, National Geographic, GEO* and *Paris-Match*. He is the winner of many prestigious awards, and has exhibited his work in London, Paris, Rome and Zurich.

Nicole Bengiveno
American/New York, New York
Bengiveno is a staff photographer for the *New York Daily News* and is associated with Matrix International. She previously worked for the *San Francisco Examiner*, and was named Bay Area Press Photographer of the Year in 1979. In 1985 she was a finalist for the W. Eugene Smith Award for her documentary work on the AIDS epidemic, and won a first place in feature photography from the New York Associated Press for her 1987 work in the Soviet Union. Recently she spent six weeks on assignment for *National Geographic* in Soviet Central Asia.

Bi Qiang
Chinese/Harbin
Bi Qiang was named one of China's ten best photographers in 1987 for his non-stop coverage of a devastating forest fire in Manchuria's Da Xing An Mountains. Today he covers the same region for the *Heilongjiang Daily*.

Torin Boyd Moscow, 1987

Torin Boyd
American/Tokyo
A veteran of five *Day in the Life* projects, Boyd began his career as a surfing photographer at the age of 17 in Cocoa Beach, Florida. Formerly a photographer for *Cocoa Today* and the *Orlando Sentinel*, he is now based in Tokyo and affiliated with Gamma Presse Images. His work currently appears in *Time, Newsweek, Life, Fortune, People, L'Express, Paris-Match* and several Japanese newsmagazines. In 1990 he will publish a calendar on Japan through Landmark Publishing.

Marilyn Bridges
American/New York, New York
After receiving an MFA degree in photography from the Rochester Institute of Technology, Bridges won both Guggenheim and Fulbright fellowships. Her work has appeared in more than 150 international exhibitions and is included in 40 major collections. She is a licensed pilot, a member of the New York Explorers Club and the author of the 1986 book, *Markings: Aerial Views of Sacred Landscapes*.

Michael Bryant
American/Philadelphia, Pennsylvania
A 1980 graduate of the University of Missouri, Bryant worked for the *San Jose Mercury News* from 1980 to 1986, during which time he was named Photographer of the Year in both California and Michigan. Now a staff photographer for the *Philadelphia Inquirer*, Bryant was a 1984 runner-up for the Pictures of the Year Portfolio.

René Burri
Swiss/Zurich
An award-winning documentary film maker, Burri has been a member of Magnum photo agency since 1956. Much of his recent photographic work on the Middle East has appeared in *Life, Stern* and the *Sunday Times* (London). The Art Institute of Chicago and the Kunsthaus in Zurich, among others, have presented solo exhibitions of his work.

Che Fu
Chinese/Beijing
Active in both the China Photojournalism Society and the Capital News Photography Society, Che has had two individual shows at the China Art Gallery in Beijing. Many of his pictures have been used in historical works both in China and abroad.

Chen Changfen
Chinese/Beijing
Born to a peasant family in Hunan, Chen now edits *Air China* magazine. A regular contributor to *People's Pictorial* and *China Photography*, he has worked as a reporter in many foreign countries. Chen currently is finishing a series of photographs on the Great Wall. Prize-winning photographs such as "Spring Breeze," "Sun and Moon" and "Meandering 5000 Kilometers" reflect his love of nature and belief that an artist's spirit must wander freely about the universe.

Paul Chesley
American/Aspen, Colorado
Chesley is a free-lance photographer who has worked with the National Geographic Society since 1975. Solo exhibitions of his work have appeared in museums in London, Tokyo and New York. China is his eighth *Day in the Life* project. His work also appears often in *Fortune, Time, GEO* and *Stern*.

Ed Cismondi, Sr.
American/Los Gatos, California
A self-taught photographer, Cismondi's first major exhibition was in 1939 at the Golden Gate International Exposition in San Francisco. Since then he has exhibited in Chicago, Los Angeles, New York and London. His work is represented in the permanent photography collections of the San Francisco Museum of Modern Art and the Oakland Museum of Art.

Bradley Clift Hartford, 1986

Bradley Clift
American/Hartford, Connecticut
A graduate of the University of Minnesota School of Journalism, Clift is now a staff photographer for the *Hartford Courant*. He is the recipient of more than 100 local, state and regional photography awards. In 1986 he won the National Press Photographers Association Photographer of the Year Award and the World Press Photo Award.

Jodi Cobb Kyoto, 1985

Jodi Cobb
American/Washington, D.C.
A graduate of the University of Missouri School of Journalism, Cobb was a photographer for the *Delaware News-Journal* and the *Denver Post* before joining the staff of *National Geographic* in 1977. She has produced five books and eleven articles. Cobb was the first woman to be voted Photographer of the Year by the White House News Photographers Association; and in 1985 she received the World Press Photo Award.

Don Cochran
American/Rochester,
New York
An Eastman Kodak staff photographer since 1981, Cochran graduated from the Rochester Institute of Technology. He is an avid nature photographer and an enthusiastic participant in such adventure sports as white-water kayaking, mountaineering and hot-air ballooning.

Dai Shunqing
Chinese/Beijing
An accomplished calligrapher and a reporter on military and police affairs for the Xinhua News Agency, Dai is a member of the China Photographers Association. He has published two books, one on the construction of the Beijing subway and the other on China's armed forces.

Jay Dickman El Salvador, 1983

Jay Dickman
American/Denver, Colorado
A 16-year veteran of the *Dallas Times Herald*, Dickman is a Denver free-lancer whose work has appeared in *Time, Life, Fortune, GEO, Bunte* and *Stern*. A recipient of the 1983 Pulitzer Prize, he won a gold medal in the World Press Photo contest and has been honored by Sigma Delta Chi, the Society of Professional Journalists.

Misha Erwitt
American/New York, New York
Erwitt has been taking pictures since he was 11 and is now on the staff of the *New York Daily News*. He has been published in *American Photographer, Esquire, People, USA Today*, and *Manhattan, inc.* Erwitt has participated in five previous *Day in the Life* projects.

Richard Eskite
American/San Francisco, California
Eskite is best known for his corporate and advertising still-life photography. He has received awards from Printing Industries of America, Inc., Consolidated Paper Companies, Inc. and the San Francisco Art Directors Club. His clients include Apple Computer, Del Monte Foods, Ghirardelli Chocolate, Levi Strauss and the Raychem Corporation.

Gerrit Fokkema
Australian/Sydney
Fokkema worked for 11 years as a staff photographer for the *Canberra Times* and the *Sydney Morning Herald*. He is now free-lancing in the corporate-industrial field.

Raphaël Gaillarde
French/Paris
Gaillarde is one of the leading news photographers of the Gamma Agency. His in-depth coverage of world news events has appeared in many European magazines, including *GEO*.

Gao Bo
Chinese/Beijing
A native of Heilongjiang, Gao won his first photography contest in 1986, but decided to sell the prize—a Hasselblad camera—to finance the beginning of his photography career. After graduating from the Central Academy of Design in Beijing with a degree in graphic arts, he turned down a state-assigned position at a publishing house to pursue a career as a free-lance photographer.

Sam Garcia
American/New York, New York
As a member of Nikon's Professional Services staff for more than 13 years, Garcia has covered most major photo events from the Kentucky Derby to four Olympics. He taught America's space shuttle astronauts how to use 35mm equipment and photographed several launches. He has worked on five previous *Day in the Life* projects, including those on Hawaii, Canada, America, Spain and California.

John Giannini
American/Hong Kong
Giannini began his career in 1969 as a US Army combat photographer in Vietnam. He has covered civil unrest and revolution in Northern Ireland, Nicaragua and the Philippines. Most recently the chief photographer for the Agence France-Presse in Beijing, he now works as a free-lancer in Hong Kong.

Diego Goldberg Germany, 1979

Diego Goldberg
Argentine/Buenos Aires
After beginning his photographic career in Latin America as a correspondent for *Camera Press*, Goldberg moved to Paris in 1977 as a Sygma staff photographer. In 1980 he moved to New York, and in 1985 returned to Argentina. His work has been featured in the world's major magazines, and in 1984 he won a World Press Photo Foundation Prize for feature photography.

Judy Griesedieck Rhode Island, 1984

Judy Griesedieck
American/San Jose, California
Griesedieck has been a staff photographer for the *San Jose Mercury News* for five years covering such events as the 1984 Democratic National Convention, the Super Bowl and the Calgary Winter Olympics. She was California Photographer of the Year in 1986, and in 1987 was the runner-up in the Canon Photo Essayist category in the University of Missouri Pictures of the Year contest. Before moving to California she was staff photographer for the *Hartford Courant*, where she was Connecticut Photographer of the Year in 1983.

Peter Haley
American/Seattle, Washington
A newspaper photographer in the Pacific Northwest for the past 10 years, Haley works for the *Morning News Tribune* in Tacoma. He was the Region 11 National Press Photographers Association Photographer of the Year in 1985, and recently participated in Collins Publishers' *Christmas in America* project.

David Alan Harvey
American/Washington, D.C.
Harvey has illustrated nearly 20 articles for *National Geographic*, and published three books. Named Magazine Photographer of the Year in 1978, he has exhibited work in the Nikon Gallery, the Museum of Modern Art in New York, the Virginia Museum of Fine Arts and Washington D.C.'s Corcoran Gallery. His photographs center on lyrical moments in everyday life, and his current book project, *Daydreamer*, will be an autobiographical reflection drawing on work from past assignments.

He Yanguang
Chinese/Beijing
Named one of China's 10 best photojournalists in 1986, He is head reporter and director of photography for *China Youth News*. He got his start in 1976, when he was arrested and jailed for seven months for taking photographs of protestors in Tiananmen Square following the death of Zhou Enlai. His experience led to his decision to become a professional photographer.

Volker Hinz
West German/New York, New York
For the past 15 years Hinz has been a staff photographer for *Stern* magazine. Based in New York since 1978, he has won many awards and traveled widely on assignment.

Huang Jingzheng
Chinese/Guangzhou
Born in Guangdong, Huang heads the photo department of the Guangdong Military District of the People's Liberation Army. Many of his photographs have appeared in *China Photography* and other magazines.

Nick Kelsh Missouri, 1978

Nick Kelsh
American/Philadelphia, Pennsylvania
A native of North Dakota, Kelsh has received numerous awards for his photos, which have appeared in *Time, Life, Newsweek, National Geographic, Forbes, Fortune* and *Business Week*. In 1986 he resigned his staff photographer position at the *Philadelphia Inquirer* to co-found Kelsh Marr Studios, a Philadelphia company which specializes in the design of and photography for annual reports and other corporate publications.

David Hume Kennerly Beijing, 1975

David Hume Kennerly
American/Los Angeles, California
A Pulitzer Prize-winning war photographer with UPI in Vietnam, Kennerly became the official White House photographer during the administration of Gerald Ford. Kennerly's experiences in Saigon and Washington are recounted in his autobiography, *Shooter*. Assignments in 125 countries have netted him 24 *Time* magazine covers. He now produces motion pictures, one of which, *The Taking of Flight 847: The Uli Dickerson Story*, was nominated for five Emmy Awards in 1988.

Douglas Kirkland
Canadian/Los Angeles, California
Kirkland is one of the world's best-known glamor and personality photographers. His 30 years in the business have included camera work with Marilyn Monroe, Marlene Dietrich, Sophia Loren and Diane Keaton. He was one of the founding members of Contact Press Images. His richly-illustrated memoir, *Lightyears,* documents his career of photographing film stars and celebrities.

Steve Krongard Sydney, 1982

Steve Krongard

American/New York, New York
One of America's top advertising and corporate photographers, Krongard's clients include American Express, British Airways, Kodak and IBM. He teaches and lectures extensively. China is his seventh *Day in the Life* project.

Jean-Pierre Laffont

French/New York, New York
Laffont attended the prestigious School of Graphic Arts in Vevey, Switzerland, prior to serving in the French army during the Algerian War. He is a founding member of the Gamma and Sygma photo agencies. He is the recipient of awards from the New York Newspaper Guild and the Overseas Press Club of America, and has received the Madelein Dane Ross Award, the World Press General Picture Award and the Nikon World Understanding Award. His work appears regularly in the world's leading news-magazines.

Frans Lanting Montana, 1986

Frans Lanting

Dutch/Santa Cruz, California
A free-lancer who works for *National Geographic*, Lanting has several books to his credit. He also has received awards in the World Press Photo Picture of the Year competition and from the American Society of Magazine Photographers.

Sarah Leen

American/Philadelphia, Pennsylvania
Leen began her career with the *Topeka Capital-Journal* and the *Philadelphia Inquirer*. She now free-lances, primarily for *National Geographic*. She is on the faculty of the University of Missouri Photo Workshop where she received honorable mention in 1986 for her story on Alzheimer's disease.

Guy Le Querrec

French/Paris
Le Querrec has traveled extensively throughout West Africa, and during the early 1970s was picture editor for *Jeune Afrique*. He co-founded the photographic cooperative Viva before joining Magnum in 1976. Though he specializes in photographing the jazz world, Le Querrec currently is putting together a book on the French region of Brittany.

Andy Levin

American/New York, New York
Born and raised in New York, Levin's pictures have appeared in a number of magazines, including *Life, People, Parade* and *National Geographic*. In 1985 and 1986 he received top honors in the National Press Photographers Association Pictures of the Year competition. A devotee of Pekingese dogs, Levin happily accepted his invitation to China, his seventh *Day in the Life* project.

Barry Lewis

British/London
With an MA from the Royal College of Art, Lewis is a founding member of the Network agency. He works for *Life, Geo*, the *Sunday Times* (London) and the *Observer*, and has photos on display in several US and British museums.

Li Binbin

Chinese/Beijing
Li became a military photographer in 1973 after five years in the army. Since 1982 his work has appeared both in China and abroad, winning more than 30 awards. He specializes in the photography of sports and daily life.

Li Qianguang

Chinese/Beijing
Li learned photography while working as a spy for the People's Liberation Army. He survived numerous reconnaissance missions against targets that still remain classified. Today he is a photographer for *PLA Pictorial*. Recently he participated in the book projects *Over China* and *The Great Wall of Iron*.

Li Weishun

Chinese/Beijing
Li took up photography upon graduation from the Naval Submarine Academy at Qingdao in 1982. Specializing in underwater subjects, he was assigned to cover the sinking of the Java Sea oil-drilling platform in 1983. A native of Shandong, he currently works as a staff photographer for the Great Wall Publishing House.

Liu Tiesheng

Chinese/Beijing
Liu's specialty is Tibet–its snow-covered mountains, its Buddhist monasteries, its many minority peoples. When not roaming his adopted home on assignment for *PLA Pictorial*, he concentrates on a more contemporary subject: China's aerospace industry.

John Loengard Ottawa, 1984

John Loengard

American/New York, New York
In 1961 Loengard joined the staff of *Life*, becoming, according to *American Photographer*, the magazine's "most influential photographer." He was the first photo editor of *People*, and in 1982 his essay on photographers, "Shooting Past 80," won first prize in the Pictures of the Year competition. He is the author of two books: *Pictures Under Discussion* and *Life Classic Photographs: A Personal Interpretation*.

Long Yunhe

Chinese/Beijing
After working 11 years as a navy publicist, Long became a professional photographer in 1980. Today, he is a photojournalist in the Political Propaganda Bureau of the Naval News Agency. He is also active in the Navy Photography Association and covers naval affairs for *PLA Pictorial*.

Gerd Ludwig Ghana, 1976

Gerd Ludwig

West German/New York, New York
A founding member of the Visum photo agency in Hamburg, Ludwig is a regular contributor to *GEO, Life, Stern, Fortune* and *Zeit Magazin*. He is an honorary member of the Deutsche Gesellschaft für Fotografie.

Ma Zengyin

Chinese/Nanjing
A career photojournalist since 1969, Ma has won more than 40 photographic medals and citations, including the People's Liberation Army's Art in Photography Award. In 1987, he was named Nanjing's Photographer of the Year. Ma has published 12 essays on photography and is a member of the China Photographers Association.

Ma Zhongyuan

Chinese/Lanzhou
A member of the Hui minority, Ma's work for the Political Department of the Lanzhou Military District of the People's Liberation Army conveys a strong flavor of China's rugged Northwest. His portraits of Gobi tribespeople, cavalry officers and soldiers have won many awards.

Mary Ellen Mark

American/New York, New York
Winner of numerous grants and awards, including the George W. Polk, Robert F. Kennedy and Phillipe Halsman awards for photojournalism, Mark has exhibited her work throughout the world, and has had photographs published in 22 books. Herself the subject of several magazine profiles, she currently contributes to *Life*, the *Sunday Times* (London), *Stern, Vanity Fair* and the *New York Times*.

Stephanie Maze

American/Washington, D.C.
Since 1979, Maze has been a free-lance photographer for *National Geographic*, working in numerous Spanish-speaking countries. Winner of several California and Washington Press Photographers awards, she has covered the Olympic games three times. Her work often appears in *GEO, People* and *Smithsonian*.

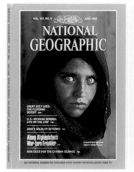

Steve McCurry Afghanistan, 1985

Steve McCurry

American/New York, New York
In 1980, McCurry's fearless coverage of the war in Afghanistan was honored with the Robert Capa Gold Medal. Since then he has won four first-place awards in the World Press Photo competition, received the Olivier Rebbot Memorial Award for his overseas photographic reporting, and been designated the 1984 Photographer of the Year by the National Press Photographers Association. A regular contributor to *National Geographic*, he is the author of the 1985 book, *The Imperial Way: Making Tracks Across India*.

Wally McNamee
American/Washington, D.C.
During his 30-year career as a photographer, McNamee has worked for the *Washington Post* and *Newsweek*, to which he has contributed more than 100 covers. He is a four-time winner of the White House News Photographers Association's Photographer of the Year Award.

Dilip Mehta Bhopal, 1987

Dilip Mehta
Canadian/Toronto
A member of Contact Press Images, Mehta has covered the Bhopal tragedy and political developments in India, Pakistan, the US and Afghanistan. His pictorial essays have been published in *Time, Newsweek, GEO, Bunte, Paris-Match, Figaro* and the *New York Times*. He has won two World Press Gold Awards and the Overseas Press Club Award.

Jim Mendenhall
American/Los Angeles, California
Mendenhall won a Pulitzer Prize for coverage of the 1984 Olympics while working for the *Orange County Register*. Now a *Los Angeles Times* staff photographer, he has published work in more than 60 magazines, including *Forbes* and *National Geographic*.

Doug Menuez Salt Lake City, 1986

Doug Menuez
American/Sausalito, California
Menuez is a free-lancer who works on assignment for *Time, Newsweek, People, Fortune, USA Today* and other publications.

Claus C. Meyer
West German/Rio de Janeiro
The winner of many prizes and awards, Meyer was selected in 1985 by *Communication World* as one of the top 10 annual-report photographers in the world. His color work has been recognized by Kodak and Nikon, and in 1981 he won a Nikon International Grand Prize. He has published several books on Brazil.

Robin Moyer
American/Hong Kong
In 1982 *Time* photographer Robin Moyer won the Press Photo of the Year Award in the World Press Photo competition and the Robert Capa Gold Medal Citation from the Overseas Press Club of America for his coverage of the war in Lebanon.

Randy Olson
American/Pittsburgh, Pennsylvania
Pittsburgh Press staff photographer Olson has won assorted regional and national awards in National Press Photographers Association contests. A University of Kansas graduate, he has free-lanced for *Fortune, US News & World Report* and *Time*. While teaching photojournalism at the University of Missouri, he received a National Archives grant for work with the Pictures of the Year Archives.

Graeme Outerbridge
Bermudian/Southampton
Named the 1985 Outstanding Young Person of the Year in Bermuda, Outerbridge is active in both politics and photography. When not working on behalf of the National Liberal Party, he submits images to *Vogue, House & Garden* and *Signature*. His first book was *Bermuda Abstracts*. A second on bridges of the world will be published in late 1989.

Bill Pierce
American/New York, New York
A Princeton graduate now working as a contract photographer for *US News & World Report*, Pierce won the 1983 Overseas Press Club's Olivier Rebbot Award for his reporting in Belfast and Beirut. A member of the Sygma photo agency, he occasionally contributes photographs to *Stern, Paris-Match, Life* and the *New York Times*.

Larry C. Price Moscow, 1987

Larry C. Price
American/Annapolis, Maryland
A native Texan who began his career with the *Fort Worth Star–Telegram* and the *El Paso Times*, Price has won two Pulitzer Prizes: in 1981 for his coverage of the Liberian coup and in 1985 for photographs taken in Angola and El Salvador. Now working for the *Philadelphia Inquirer*, Price has been honored by the Overseas Press Club, World Press Photo and the National Press Photographers Association.

Eli Reed
American/New York, New York
Reed followed up a 1982 Nieman Fellowship with a 1983 Pictures of the Year Nikon World Understanding Award for his coverage of Central America. In 1988 he published *Beirut, City of Regrets*. Recent projects include a documentary film on poverty among children and a forthcoming photo essay on Black America.

Roger Ressmeyer California, 1988

Roger Ressmeyer
American/San Francisco, California
A Yale graduate and the founder of the Starlight Photo Agency, Ressmeyer is one of America's leading aerospace photographers. He is also known for his portraiture and his photos appear on book jackets and record album covers. Between *Day in the Life* projects, he contributes to *Smithsonian, Discover* and *Air & Space* magazines.

Jim Richardson
American/Denver, Colorado
Richardson is a free-lance photographer whose images often appear in *Time, Fortune* and *National Geographic*. His photography of small-town life in the American Midwest has been honored at the World Understanding Contest with three Special Recognition Awards.

Rick Rickman Des Moines, 1983

Rick Rickman
American/Santa Ana, California
During the five years he worked for the *Des Moines Register*, Rickman was named Iowa Photographer of the Year three times. In 1985, he brought a Pulitzer Prize in Spot News Photography to the *Orange County Register*, and was chosen California Photographer of the Year.

Joe Rossi
American/St. Paul, Minnesota
Rossi grew up in Bemidji, Minnesota, and worked for the *Marshall Independent* and the *Worthington Daily Globe* before joining the *St. Paul Pioneer Press & Dispatch* in 1983.

Sebastião Salgado
Brazilian/Paris
Fluent in four languages, Salgado holds advanced degrees in economics from Vanderbilt University and the University of Paris. But in 1973, after witnessing the misery of the drought-plagued African Sahel, he stopped writing technical reports and began capturing dramatic images. His coverage of war and famine focuses on the humanitarian needs of society's weakest victims.

Paul Christopher Sancya
American/Gary, Indiana
A professional photographer for the past two years, Sancya's attendance at an Eddie Adams Workshop led to an assignment for *National Geographic* and an invitation to experience *A Day in the Life of China*.

George Steinmetz
American/San Francisco, California
Before graduating from Stanford University with a degree in geophysics, Steinmetz took two and a half years to hitchhike through more than 20 African countries. His work currently appears in *Fortune, Life, National Geographic* and the *New York Times Magazine*.

Patrick Tehan
American/Santa Ana, California
A photo published in *A Day in the Life of America* earned Tehan top honors in the magazine division of the National Press Photographers Association's Pictures of the Year competition. In 1981, he was named a regional Photographer of the Year. He presently works for the *Orange County Register*.

Neal Ulevich Beijing, 1986

Neal Ulevich
American/Tokyo
Ulevich recently completed a four-and-a-half-year assignment in China as an Associated Press photographer and photo editor. He has spent two decades in Asia, and won the Pulitzer Prize in 1977 for photographs of anti-leftist rioting in Thailand. He currently works as Asia Communications Manager for AP.

Jerry Valente
American/New York, New York
Valente specializes in corporate and industrial photography. When not pursuing editorial assignments, he helps run a New York food bank.

Wang Miao
Chinese/Beijing
A photographer for *China Tourism* magazine in Hong Kong, Wang's most evocative photo study, "Poems Collected from the Open Country," was published in 1982 by *China Photography* magazine. She was a principal contributor to the commemorative photo album, *Grief of the People*, which conveys the depth of sorrow that followed the death of Zhou Enlai in 1976.

Wang Wenlan
Chinese/Beijing
Wang is director of photography at the *China Daily*, China's only English-language newspaper. His dramatic photos of the bloody protests in Tiananmen Square following the 1976 death of Zhou Enlai were followed by equally evocative images of the Tangshan earthquake. Today, Wang lectures, organizes photography conferences and sits on the board of the China Photographers Association.

Dan White
American/Kansas City, Missouri
White was born in Michigan and educated at the University of Missouri. The author of a book called *Independence*, he worked for several newspapers before joining a Pulitzer Prize-winning team at the *Kansas City Star*. His company, White & Associates, accepts editorial and corporate assignments.

Wu Jinsheng
Chinese/Beijing
Born in Liaoning, Wu took up photography as a teenager and later studied cinematography at the Beijing Film Institute. He joined *PLA Pictorial* as a staff photographer in 1973. Since then, his photo essays have received numerous awards and have been exhibited throughout China.

Wu Shouzhuang
Chinese/Beijing
An accomplished aerial photographer, Wu has logged nearly 700 hours in fighter jets and other military aircraft. His pictures have appeared in such magazines as *PLA Pictorial*, *International Aviation* and *Air Force Today*. Unfortunately, some of his best work remains classified for purposes of national defense.

Wu Zhiyi
Chinese/Beijing
A 1977 graduate of the Nanjing College of Engineering, Wu was selected as one of China's 10 best photographers. A member of both the China Photographers Association and the China Contemporary Photography Society, Wu specializes in military and sports subjects. He recently held a one-man show at the China Art Gallery.

Xu Zhigang
Chinese/Shanghai
Born in Taiwan, Xu now works for the Shanghai Educational Publishing House. His photos have appeared in *China Photography*, *People's Daily*, *Popular Photography* and many foreign publications. One of Xu's photos, "Sacred Rights," received first-place honors in the One Billion People Photography Competition sponsored by the *China Daily*.

Yang Changzhong
Chinese/Beijing
Yang is one of China's best sports photographers. A staff photographer for *New Sports* magazine, he received top honors in the 1983 World Sports Photography competition.

Yang Dan
Chinese/Beijing
During the Cultural Revolution, Yang worked as a flutist in the orchestra of a song and dance troupe. Later, he became a barefoot doctor. But his love of art and visual images attracted him to photography, and in 1983 he enrolled in photography courses at People's University. Upon graduation, he joined the staff of *Forestry Pictorial*. Today he works at *China Forestry News*.

Yang Shaoming
Chinese/Beijing
Son of two veterans of the Long March, Yang was an amateur photographer for 20 years before joining the Xinhua News Agency in 1979. His first book, on the Great Snowy Mountains and Grasslands, was published in 1981.

Yang Xiaolu
Chinese/Beijing
Trained at People's University, Yang is the head photographer for *China Postal Service* magazine. A new member of the China Photographers Association, he has published his work in Zambia, Nigeria and France. Recently five of his photos were exhibited during the International Symposium on Rural Postal Work.

Yuan Xuejun China, 1986

Yuan Xuejun
Chinese/Beijing
Though a reporter for the *PLA Pictorial*, Yuan is best-known for his evocative photos of village life. Selected as one of China's 10 best photographers in 1987, he has received more than 80 awards in international photo competitions.

Zhang Tongsheng
Chinese/Beijing
Zhang is a photographer for the government's Committee on Defense, Science, Technology and Industry. His award-winning photo studies of wind tunnels, rocket-launching pads and iron foundries have been exhibited in Hong Kong, France and Romania. He is also the photographer, editor and publisher of the photo album, *China's Defense Technology Research and Development*.

Zhao Zhonglu
Chinese/Chengdu
Zhao is editor in chief of *War Flag Report*, a publication of the Chengdu Military District. His photographs appear in the large-format book, *Monument to the Red Army*, and have been featured in dozens of exhibitions.

Zhou Yi
Chinese/Beijing
A photojournalist for the Great Wall Publishing House, Zhou was honored in 1987 for 30 years of service as a military photographer. His pictures have appeared in dozens of magazines and several books, including *Chinese Troops Today* and *Collections of History*.

Zhu Xianmin
Chinese/Beijing
Zhu edits both *China Photographer* and *China Photography* magazines. In 1988 a retrospective of his work was published by the People's Fine Arts Publishing Company. In 1985, his photographs were featured in a China Art Gallery exhibition which traveled to Henan, Jilin, Jiangsu and Zhu's native Shandong. In addition to his work with the China Photographers Association, Zhu also serves as director of the Exhibitions Committee of the China Photojournalism Society.

This book was designed and produced entirely on an Apple Macintosh II computer equipped with a SuperMac Trinitron monitor and three DataFrame XP-60 hard-disc drives. The images were digitized with a Barneyscan and an Abaton 300. Output was generated on a Linotronic 300 printer. Project software included Aldus PageMaker, Adobe Illustrator '88, Living Videotext's MORE and Microsoft Works. Collins Publishers has a local area network utilizing Farallon Computing's PhoneNET PLUS and THINK Technology's INBOX to link 15 Macintoshes. We gratefully acknowledge the companies listed above for their assistance.

Additional Photo Credits
Page 1: Photographed by
Jim Mendenhall, USA

Pages 2-3: Photographed by
Peter Haley, USA

Pages 12-13: Photographed by
Graeme Outerbridge, Bermuda

Pages 14-15: Photographed by
Richard Eskite, USA

Pages 208-209: Photographed by
Doug Menuez, USA

Page 221: Photographed by
Patrick Tehan, USA

Pages 222-223: Photographed by
Frans Lanting, Netherlands

Page 224: Photographed by
Rick Rickman, USA

Project Staff

Editor & Project Director
David Cohen

General Manager
Jennifer Erwitt

Managing Editor
Mark Rykoff

Art Director
Jennifer Barry

Writer
David DeVoss

Publicity Director
Patti Richards

Sponsorship Director
Cathy Quealy

Production Director
Stephanie Sherman

Assignment Editors
Martha Avery
Bill Messing

Travel Director
Kate Kelly

Office Manager
Linda Lamb

Production Coordinator
Kathryn Yuschenkoff

Assistant Art Director
Charles Tyrone

Production Assistant
Monica Baltz

Assistant Managing Editor
O. David Spitzler

Logistics Coordinator
James Kordis

Copy Editors
Dana Sachs
Jonathan A. Schwartz

Picture Editors

Sandra Eisert
San Jose Mercury News

Alfonso Gutiérrez Escera
A.G.E. Fotostock

Peter Howe
Life Magazine

Eliane Laffont
Sygma

Michele McNally
Fortune Magazine

Dieter Steiner
Stern Magazine

Michele Stephenson
Time Magazine

Susan Vermazen
New York Magazine

George Wedding
Sacramento Bee

Associate Picture Editor
George Olson

**Photography & Design
Consultants**

Robert Pledge
Contact Press Images

Michael Rand
The Sunday Times (London)

Sponsorship Consultant
John Johns

Travel Consultant
Karen Bakke

Publishing Adviser
Oscar Dystel

China Consultants
Stephen FitzGerald
Peter Forsythe
Clare Fearnley
*Stephen FitzGerald & Co.
Canberra/Beijing*

Attorneys
E. Gabriel Perle
*Proskauer, Rose, Goetz &
Mendelsohn*

William Coblentz
*Coblentz, Cahen, McCabe &
Breyer*

Collins Publishers

**Director of Finance and
Administration**
Stanford Hays

Sales Director
Carole Bidnick

Accounting Manager
Peter Smith

Assistant Sales Director
Brian Hajducek

Senior Accountant
Jenny Collins

Assistant to the President
John Clay Stites

Administrative Assistants
Ruth Jacobson
Tom LeBeau

**Weldon Owen Publishing
Limited**

President
John Owen

Project Coordinator
Anne Greensall

Beijing Coordinators
Harold Weldon
Robert Cave-Rogers

Administration
Vivien Griffiths

Finance Manager
Stanley Chan

Dai Nippon Printing Co., Ltd.

Ryo Chigira
Fujio Ojima
Kosuke Tago
Kikuo Mori
Mitsuo Gunji
Yoshiyasu Kosugi
Kimio Honda

Collins Sales Representatives

Mid-Atlantic
Robert Eickemeyer
John Leibfried
Bert Lippincott, Jr.

Midwest
Leah Berg
Jim Lauber
Gene Rotenberg

Mountain States
Gordon Saull

New England
Joan Emery
Marc Seager

Southeast
John Genovese
Mike Lamers
Edward Springer
Edward Wood, Jr.

Southwest
Theron Palmer, Jr.
Theron Palmer, Sr.
Chuck Weeth

West Coast
Robert Ditter
Ted Lucia
William Maher
Thomas McFadden
Judy Wheeler

Sponsors and Contributors

Sponsors
Eastman Kodak
   Company
Nikon Inc.
Northwest Airlines, Inc.
BankAmerica Corp.
   WorldMoney
   Travelers Cheques
Holiday Inn Lido, Beijing
Federal Express
   Corporation

Major Contributors
Apple Computer, Inc.
Atoztec Systems Ltd.
British Airways
Farallon Computing, Inc.
Holiday Inn Harbour
   View, Hong Kong
Hyatt Regency
   San Francisco
The New Lab
Pallas Photo Labs, Inc.
Pan American World
   Airways
United Airlines

Contributors
Abaton
Adobe Systems
Aldus Corporation
Arch
Avalon Development
   Group
Barneyscan Corporation
Beijing Television
CAAC Guangzhou
Chengdu Military
   Command
Chengdu Military Dist.
   Logistics Department
Cherry Hill Travel,
   Denver
China Central Television
China Cultural Printing
   Company
China Daily
China Youth News
Connect Information
   Service
Dynamac Computer
   Products, Inc.
E-Machines
Eagle Creek Travel Gear
Episode Inc.
G Engraving
Gansu Military District
   Political Department
The Great Hall of the
   People
Great Wall Mansions,
   Guangzhou
Guangdong Foreign
   Affairs Office
Guangdong Press &
   Publishing Authority
Guangdong Publishing
   Import/Export Co.
Guangming Daily
Guangxi Military District
   Political Department

Guilin Clock & Camera
   Company
Guilin Municipal
   Government
Guizhou Minorities
   Publishing House
HI-FI
Hilton International Hotel,
   Tokyo
Huayuan Technology Co.
Infomax Computers
JC Supply
Jebsen Travel, Hong Kong
Jinjiang Hotel, Shanghai
Krishna Copy Center
Lanzhou Military District
   Political & Propaganda
   Departments
Lanzhou Silk Mill
Lindblad Travel, Inc.
Linxia Military
   Subdistrict
Living Videotext, Inc.
Lundeen Associates
M & H Travel, Inc.,
   New York
Microsoft Corporation
Morrison A Travel
   Corporation, San Mateo
National University of
   Defense & Technology
Omnicomp
PMG Marketing
Pacrim Technologies
Panalpina Inc.
People's Daily
Personal Training Systems
Primal Screen
PrintMasters
Publish!
Qinzhou Municipal
   Government
Quark Inc.
Radius Inc.
Release 1.0
Rucker Fuller
Samy's Camera
San Francisco Giants
San Francisco Public
   Library, Chinatown Branch
San Francisco Public
   Library, Main Branch
San Francisco Services
   Word Processing
Shanghai Conservatory
   of Music
Shanghai Municipal
   Government Foreign
   Affairs Office
Shanghai Press &
   Publishing Authority
Shanghai Translation
   Publishing House
Silicon Beach Software
Smith Novelty Company
Sony Corporation of
   America
SuperMac Technologies
Symantec Corporation,
   THINK Technologies
   Division
Track Industries
The Understanding Business
UC Berkeley Center for
   Chinese Studies Library
Visas Unlimited
Working People's
   Cultural Palace Park
Wuqiao Acrobatics School

Friends, Advisers and Consultants
Eddie Adams
John Alfano
Jeff Allen
Rennie Allinger
An Lerong
Charles Anderson
Perso Androus
Peter Angelis
M. Aoki
Bill Atkinson
Mark Avery
Ba Yi'er
Chriss Babbitt
Bai Shi
Anna Maria Bambara
Peter Bamburg
Susan Barnes
Howard Barney
Lori Barra
Susan Barton
Brent Baskfield
Jeanne Bayer
David Bell
Chuck Bennett
Bill Berry
Roger Bishop
Gene Blumberg
Phillip Blumenthal
Julie Boerger
Mike Boich
Amy Bonatti
Liz Bond
Timothy James Bond
Jim Bonde
Ralf Borchert
Jeff Bork
Emily Boxer
Emily Boyles
Paul Brainerd
Diana Bray
Kandes Bregman
Abbe Brod
John Brown
Russell Brown
Rick Brunelle
Laury Bryant
Rudy Burger
Sandy Burton
Cai Heping
Claire Calanog
Woody Camp
Bill Campbell
Cao Li
Cao Zili
Denise Caruso
Jerry Cassel
Dr. Frank Catchpool
Mike & Gina Cerre
Dave Chambers
Benny Chan
Clement Chan
Brad Chaney
Clarence Chang
Chang Lin
Ian & Marjorie Chapman
Howard Chapnick
Sarah Charf
Bruce Charonnat
C.P. Chen
Chen Hao
Chen Hui
Chen Jing
Chen Juming

Chen Linrong
Chen Ningsheng
Chen Rongfei
Chen Shaoyong
Chen Xi
Chen Xiangxue
Chen Xiaoyong
Chen Xuwei
Chen Yingfu
Chen Yixin
Cheng Xifeng
Masnik Cheong
Gary Cheung
Chi Guangming
Gilbert Chow
Judy Ann Christensen
Arta Christiansen
Dale & June Christiansen
Albert Chu
Laurence Chu
June Chui
Beth Churchill-Fantz
A.B. Clausen
Susan Clevenger
George Coates
Daniel Cohen
Kara Cohen
Norman & Hannah
   Cohen
Steven & Ellyn Cohen
William G.K. Cohen
Lew Coleman
Chuck & Paula Collins
Sandy Colton
Vicky Comiskey
Sue Contois
Lisa Court
Elinor Craig
Cui Jin
Fred Daley
Dan Zeng
Paula David
Tony & Malka David
Bob Davis
Jim Davis
Craig Dawson
Ed Deal
Cliff Deeds
Al de Guzman
Deng Zijian
Marci Dickey
Ding Lianfang
Chickie Dioguardi
Grant Ditzler
Kevin Doherty
Dong Dejian
Debbie Donnelly
Sheila Donnelly
Bob Doughty
Lynne T. Doyle
Arnold H. Drapkin
Gene & Gayle Driskell
Hugh Dubberly
Kristin Dukay
Mark Dunaway
Dick Duncan
Esther Dyson
Lois Eagleton
Fred Ebrahimi
Steve Edelman
Lisa Edmondson
Will & Liz Edwards
Dr. & Mrs. Richard
   Eisenberg
Ken Ellis
Ron Enriquez
Jeffrey & Susan Epstein
Ellen Erwitt
Elliott Erwitt

Gordon Eubanks
Jane Everingham
Collette Evrard
Fan Jie
Fang Hui
Fang Wei
Daniel Farber
Craig Farnum
Jason Farrow
Phil Feldman
Harlan Felt
Feng Chunqi
Lisa Ferdinandsen
Bran Ferren
James Ferri
Roy Fidler
Paolo E. Fill
Dana Fineman
Jaime FlorCruz
Bob Fournier
Jim Frey
Rolf Fricke
Fu Jiangning
Dickson Fung
Thomas Fung
Gan Bo
Gao Feng
Jean Louis Gassee
Ursula Gauthier
Ge Pengren
Deborah Gee
Ed Gencarelli
Geng Qinghua
Geng Quanli
Kathy Georgette
Karen Gerold
Mike Giles
Brendon Gill
Bill Giordano
Danny Goodman
John Graham
Bruce W. Gray
Brian Grazer
George Green
Keith Green
Michael J. Greene
Lisa Gregory
Stephen Gregory
Guan Chongsheng
Susan Gubernat
Connie Guglielmo
Gui Dingkui
Gui Jianhua
Guo Min
David & Susan Hagerman
Barbara Hahn
Hai Yuanbao
Richard Handl
Meredith Hankey
Nick Harris
Pam Harrison
Ernie Haskin
Steve Haugen
Jean Hazelwood
He Cheng
He Fenglong
He Wenjie
He Zhide
François Hebel
Steve Heier
Hugh Helm
Tina Helsell
Linda Hering
Otilia Hernandez
Andy Hertzfeld
James Higa
Lynette Hinton
Harry Hoffman
Sam Hoffman

Alison Hofland
Mike Holm
Hong Mei
Hong Minsheng
Ritchie Horowitz
Hou Jingli
Pat Howlett
Hu Qian
Hu Shanwen
Dede Huang
Erwin Huang
Huang Fuwang
Huang Gongqing
Huang Pingxian
Huang Qun
Huang Xi
Huang Ximan
Dave Hudson
Carmond Hui
Quinssy Hung
George Hurd
Bill Hurst
Fred Hykal
Yuichi Inomata
Ranny Ip
Miyuki Ishii
Vern Iuppa
Charlie Jackson
Janice James
Todd James
Joanne Jaulus
Krissy Jensen
Prof. Jia Xiangzhang
Jiang Xiangning
Steve Jobs
Tom W. Johnson
Kathy Jones
Cecil Juanarena
Madelyn Kahn
Anna Kamdar
Devyani Kamdar
Mira Kamdar
P.P. Kamdar
Pravin & Caroline
  Kamdar
Susan Kare
Cynthia Kasabian
Troy Kashon
Betty & Fred Kauffman
Dr. Richard & Marianne
  Kelly
Susan Kelly
Bob Kennedy
Michael Kennedy
Tom Kennedy
Ron Key
Brad Kibbel
Cherie Kilby
Douglas J. King
Françoise Kirkland
Glenn Knowlton
Kent Kobersteen
John B.T. Kong
Tony Krantz
Gino Kremple
Jeff Kriendler
Andrew Kruger
Joseph H. Kushner
Ben Kwan
Kenny Kwok
David LaDuke
Wendy Lagerstrom
Mr. & Mrs. Stuart Lamb
John Lampl
Sonia Land
Bill Lane
May Law
Le Junlun
Frances Lee

Rudi Legname
Robert Golden Leigh
Patti Lepa
Catherine Leung
Charles Leung
Mindy Leventhal
Richard Levick
Martin Levin
Mr. & Mrs. James
  Levinson
Li Dong
Li Haicheng
Li Haidong
Li Jianqi
Li Jianxing
Li Jiaxin
Li Jie
Li Qirui
Li Shengwen
Li Wei
Li Xiaorong
Li Yazhou
Li Zhongmin
Liang Caoxing
Liang Zechao
Lin Lin
Lin Yongjun
Cedric Ling
Ling Zifeng
Liu Fahui
Liu Guozhen
Liu Jingshan
Liu Jingtang
Joseph Liu
Liu Peide
Liu Renyi
Liu Wenwei
Liu Zhong
Mr. & Mrs. Edward
  Lloyd
Tom & Susan Lloyd
Simon Lo
Stan Loll
Bonnie Lopata
Arsenio Lopez
Geraldine Lopez
Richard LoPinto
Sonja Lorberg
Barbara Loren
Lou Chaotian
Lou Zhaotian
Wesley Lowe
Whitney Lowe
Lu Hongyan
Lu Jinkun
Lu Tongju
Luan Zhengyuan
Tim Lundeen
Ma Ling
Judi Magann
A.B. Magary
Chris Majoy
Alfred Mandel
Emily Manwaring
Mao Yandong
Thom Marchionna
Bill Markovich
Anja Marquardt
Bob Marshall
Wendy Marzetta
Sue Mason
Mahmood Masood
Dixie Matthews
Lucienne & Richard
  Matthews
Ernst Mayer
Holloway McCandless
Laurie McClean

Charles McElroy
Pat McEvoy
D. Pat McGuire
Kevin McVea
Stan Mencher
Cathy Menconi
Meng He
Meng Zhaorui
Walter & Judy Miller
Nancy Miscia
Jim Mitchell
Clement Mok
Marlene Morgan
Ann Moscicki
Sue Moss
Prof. Hua-Yuan Li
  Mowry
Hiroshi Nakamura
Claude Nederovique
Ni Fagui
Nie Zhiming
Nick Nishida
Shirley Norton
Colleen Norvell
Mohamed Noureldin
Sidney Oakes
Cameron Ong
Brian O'Reilly
Gene Ostroff
Ou Shun'an
Carrie Padilla
Rusty Pallas
Rick Pappas
Irene M. Park
Margaret Pau
Daniel Paul
Bill Pekala
Peng Haokun
Peng Xuemei
Tyler Peppel
Liz Perle
Mario Perrone
Alec & Ann Petersen
Jeff Peterson
Mike Phillips
Paul Phillipson
Roger Pisani
Chris Pitsaris
Debbie Plant
Tom Plaskett
Alan Poon
Rebel Price
Darcy Provo
Paul Pruneau
Pu Zenghua
Qi Kejun
Qi Xin
Qiao Jianping
Qin Liying
Qiu Yue
Cherie Quaintance
Dr. Robert Rapkin
Suzanne Raulston
Teresa Reichensperger
Gary Reid
Marta Remenius
Ren Jianwen
Ron Rhody
Vanessa Rice
Bernd Riegger
Thomas P. Rielly
Betty Riess
Cornel & Susan Riklin
Jeannie Rodgers
Manuel J. Rodriguez
Rong Yiren
Ben Rose
David Rose
Joan & Bob Rosenberg

Alain Rossman
David Rousseau
Dan Ruben
Richard & Anica
  Rushton
Pat Ryan
Paul Saffo
Nola Safro
Scott & Eao Sagan
Sanjay Sakhuja
Mark Salzman
Bill Samenko
Marianne Samenko
Curt Sanborn
Will & Marta Sanburn
Sang Ye
Lilla Sanullo
Kerilyn Sappington
Ariane Starpa
Dick Schaap
Steve Schaffren
Fred Scherrer
Ricky Schlessinger
Paul Schnidman
Madalyn Schmidt
Linda Schrack
Kaiulani Schuler
Marie Schuman
Julie Scott
John Sculley
Neil & Karen Shakery
Bob Shakebrook
Shen Chen
Shen Genzi
Eleanor Sherman
Steven & Danan
  Sherman
Shi Liwen
Shi Yang
Shi Yunzheng
Sandy Skinbo
K. Shioir
Judith Shmueli
Joan Simms
Mark Simon
Andrew Singer
Bob Siroka
Lorrie Sisca
Doug Sleeter
Sylvia Slaight
Burrell Smith
David Smith
Joanne Smith
Marvin & Gloria Smolan
Song Huaigui
Song Weide
Andree Soscia
Michael Spedale
Pete Spence
Ruth F. Spitzler
Lee Sporn
Randy Springer
Donald H. Stang
John Stevenson
Andy Stewart
Jim Stockton
Michael Story
Bob Stovall
Lew Stowbunenko
Joe Strea
Steve Streeter
John Stum
Y. Sudo
Ben Sugaya
Sun Geq
Sun Jian
Sun Xinhua
Sun Xuezhen
Sun Yaoqing

Peter Sutch
Nancy Swanson
Kiyomi Takeyama
Kathy Tallone
Jon Tandler
Tang Nianzu
Tang Xue
Tang Zhenhuang
Joe Targett
Michael Tchao
Karen Teitelbaum
John Temple
Michael Tette
Victoria Theile
Jordan Thorn
Tian Aijun
Milton To
Doug Tompkins
Neil Topham
Bill Tracy
Sue Trevaskas
Tu Zhongliang
Karen Tucker
Susan Tuller
Vea Van Kessel
Louis Vivas
Judy Walsh
Wan Zhengming
Wan Zhixian
Wang Bo
Wang Boyu
Wang Chunyuan
Wang Jing
Wang Lihong
Wang Ping
Wang Xiangen
Wang Xiangshen
Wang Xinmin
Wang Yong
Wang Yonghong
Wang Yuwei
Wang Zheng
John Warnock
Wei Hongyan
Wei Jianmin
Gretchen Weinstein
Michael Wellman
Susan Wels
Wen Shaojun
Weng Yongqin
Eric Weyenberg
Dick Wien
Kathy Wilhelm
Robin Williams
T. Andrew Wilson
Dave Winer
Gary Wintz
Miriam Wittig
David Wong
Elsie Lee Wong
Trevor Wong
William Wong
Louis Woo
Jim & Sarah Woods
Peter Workman
Simon Worrin
Harmony Wu
Wu Changhua
Wu Deyin
Wu Xiaonu
Richard Saul Wurman
Xia Daoling
Xiang Lin
Xiao Guo
Xiao Hu
Xiao Jinghua
Xing Yuchun
Xu Dongyu
Xu Liyi

Xu Mulin
Xu Senyuan
Xu Yuanni
Xu Yuquan
Xu Zhijian
Yan Xinshu
Belle Yang
Yang Guanming
Yang Shizhong
Wendy Yang
Yang Xishan
Yang Xishun
Yang Zunian
Celina Yannucci
Yao Ligong
Ye Menhua
Ye Xi
Bob Yeager
Rebecca Yeung
Vireo Yeung
Yi Zhihong
Ying Ruocheng
T. Yoshioka
You Liping
You Yong
Dean Younger
Paul Yu
Yu Ping
Bill Yuen
Michael & Dorothea
  Yuschenkoff
Carol Zanutto
Zhang Aiping
Zhang Bin
Zhang Bingming
Zhang Fushou
Zhang Guangdong
Zhang Guochao
Prof. Zhang Heci
Zhang Lei
Zhang Lihua
Zhang Longdong
Zhang Ming
Zhang Shaohong
Zhang Wei
Zhang Weicheng
Zhang Weili
Zhang Xianliang
Zhang Xiuqiao
Zhang Xiuyun
Zhang Xuanda
Zhang Xuejun
Zhang Zihua
Zhao Guohua
Zhao Hongdou
Zhao Huiyuan
Zhao Laixiang
Zhao Liguo
Zhao Meili
Raymond Zhao
Zhao Yunhuai
Zhou Kairi
Zhou Li
Zhu Huasheng
Zhu Weigen
Zhu Yifan
Zhu Yinghuang
Zhu Yingnan
Zhu Zhenming
Zhuang Jian
Ernst Zimmerman
Orlando Zuniga
Brandon Zurlo

Special thanks to
Raymond H. DeMoulin

Warm appreciation to
Rick Smolan

Thank you to the People of China.